Brisby, Barbara C

PLAY AND MENTAL HEALTH

PLAY AND MENTAL HEALTH

Principles and Practice for Teachers

BY
JOHN EISELE DAVIS, M.A.
Veterans' Administration Facility, Perry Point, Md.
Author of
PRINCIPLES AND PRACTICES OF RECREATIONAL THERAPY
FOR THE MENTALLY ILL

NEW YORK
A. S. BARNES AND COMPANY
1938

To My Parents

*Whose love and understanding of life made
happy the early excursions into play.*

CONTENTS

ACKNOWLEDGEMENTS

In this endeavor, the author desires to acknowledge with gratitude valued assistance and encouragement from many sources.

Dr. Adolf Meyer has supplied the vital spark of encouragement and many of his illuminating suggestions have provided the spirit of the general approach to the problems of play in a more natural hygienic setting. Dr. William R. Dunton has given many practical lessons of the pregnant relationship of psychiatric principles to play method. Dr. Frederick L. Patry has examined part of the manuscript most carefully and suggested amplifications which have added to its comprehensiveness and more effective relationship to psychiatric temper and method. Educational implications have been critically perused by Dr. Frederick L. Livingood who has made suggestions in the light of the modern trend of teaching. Acknowledgement is made of indebtedness to the late Dr. William A. White especially for many suggestions from his "Mental Hygiene of Childhood." Margaret H. Wagenhals has rendered most helpful assistance in going over much of the manuscript and adding valued suggestions.

Grateful acknowledgement is made to The American Psychiatric Association, The National Committee for Mental Hygiene, The American Physical Education Association and The American Occupational Therapy Association for permission to use material from their publications.

FOREWORD

AN UNUSUALLY successful and clear headed worker and writer on recreational therapy for the mentally ill gives us a counterpart of prevention in "Play and Mental Health for the Child." A philosophy in terms of action and experience is put before the reader, with unusual cleverness and ease of diction. A boon to the children and to teachers, these pages will be a great help to the physician as well, and to all those who as therapists have to replace what often is more mistake than structural disease, and what even in structural disease is best reached and redirected to sound performance and health.

May wide recognition and use reward the author.

ADOLF MEYER

March 19, 1937.

INTRODUCTION

I AM ATTEMPTING HERE to present the subject of play as usable material for the organization of effective mental hygienic practises in school and to this end to develop a psychology of play in line with the spirit and the recent advances of psychiatric practises in child education.

It is fundamental to consider how disorderly and difficult is the struggle of the child toward maturity. He is expected to transform himself in a very short time from an egocentric animal into a socialized being, not only assimilating the refinements of rigid social mores but accepting with grace these confusing superimposed restrictions. He must gradually cast aside the strong primitive urges which so powerfully drive him to live and to love in unconventional and even strange ways. He most frequently resents this and in spite of our heavy teaching casts longingly for an expansive rather than a restrictive temper of teaching. The abstract concepts of socialization are through training impressed upon him and with growth and understanding, he experiences the feeble beginnings of a desire to leave the crowd for the community, so to speak, and also the strong antagonistic yearning to go back to the crowd. Such conflicting and alternate desires become colored by emotional and volitional concomitants and these early experiences become heavily charged with psychic energy in which educational control becomes imperative. The conflict between self-love and adherence to so-called higher altruistic formulations persists through life.

This process of social transmutation as well as the generally accepted formal procedures are becoming the increasing responsibility of modern education. Organic or functional trauma often interfere with this orderly process and many maladjusted children present, as a result, complex behaviour problems for the teacher.

The child tells the story of his life in his activity. He desires to control it and to fashion it so that he may present a picture of himself acceptable both to his fellows and to his own personality. While he attempts to interpret his environment through his activity he is more concerned with the interpretation of himself and to this end he seeks a sympathetic medium, an expansive type of activity, an experience which will allow expression of his innate as well as formalized yearnings and desires many of which are so unconventional that he dare not divulge them, longings which have become repressed, aspirations which have been postponed in the confusion which has resulted from the revaluation of early desires under the pressure of the higher demands of altruistic aims. In this situation, the child seeks something likeable and interesting, a dynamic experience with the characteristic of modifiability so that he can use it, change it and reshape it until it conforms to his purpose and ideal.

Play is this modifiable experience which in the hands of the child and the hygienically trained teacher possesses so many elements out of which to organize and project lessons vitally related to the child's most effective growth and wholesome development. Among the many contributions of play there are two most significant fundamentals of wholesome personality adjustment: a, the delicate element of interest so necessary to valid educational effort; b, a sense of individual worthwhileness and personal security evoked through the rational development of motor skills. This utilization of the sensory level as a basis for the modification of mental attitudes is a most important objective of modern mental hygiene.

The hygienically conscious teacher will study the whole personality of the child rather than the purely physical aspects of education. While the big muscle activities are acknowledged to be fundamental and, therefore, most important; personality factors which emerge from the intellectual, emotional, volitional and social levels should be carefully considered. Conduct is viewed as a unity, an integration of all these personality attributes, the physical as well as the mental.

The modern teacher will extend her frontiers of interest and inquiry into the newer psychological fields which aim to explore the increasingly entrancing phenomena of conduct. It may not be too much to request that the teacher make a study of some of the fundamental psychiatric concepts which aim to more critically evaluate behaviour such as the concept of the oedipus, electra, and castration conflicts, sadism, masochism, emotional fixation, regression, complexes of inferiority and superiority, the theoretical concepts of psychoanalysis. An elemental understanding of these mechanisms of conduct will assist in the more effective utilization of play in education.

One cannot overly simplify mental mechanisms without loss of definite clarity. At the present stage of interest and understanding it appears advisable to call attention to the more clearly nucleated principles of mental hygiene in their possible application to education in play. These applications have been sought in the familiar and even old fashioned types and characteristics of play. There has been no attempt to present a scientific formulation nor to claim a rigorous scientific method. An endeavor has been made to propound a general philosophy of play which may be conducive to wholesome mental expression, growth and development leading to socialized behaviour which is best attained through the educational integration of our mental and bodily processes.

PLAY AND MENTAL HEALTH

Chapter I

PLAY

AND PSYCHIC

ADJUSTMENT

A COOPERATIVE AND COMPETITIVE EXPERIENCE

THE CONCEPT OF A GAME as the zestful action of the child playing in friendly intercourse with rather than against other children invests it with the highest hygienic usefulness. As a way of pleasurable social behaving, play will find its most helpful relationship to educational practice. The popular concept, however, is far removed from such an ideal yet practical aim. Many consider struggle and dominance of one individual against another as providing the inherent zest and spirit. The child through education and environment has been led to find his greatest satisfaction out of the fighting aspect of his play experiences. The detrimental influences of such a narrow and distorted viewpoint are apparent in the unsatisfactory adjustment of the child not only to play but to many other relationships.

The teacher who observes the child at play is at once impressed with the all-powerfulness of the ideal of competition. He seems keenly desirous and even acutely anxious to overcome something or someone. The experience to him most frequently represents a struggle with an opponent and a severe vying for mastery may most naturally lead to combative other than cooperative conduct. And this is not strange for the American motif most frequently espoused is advancement through competition and struggle. The observant parent, schooled in this American system, unthinkingly approves and probably enjoys the racy quality of sharp rivalry and its peppery competitive tang. "My boy is real," he explains in self-sufficient praise, "he will fight for his rights, and anything I despise is a sickening mawkish play spoiled by the absence of real fighting spirit." And he probably finds historical justification for this viewpoint as the motif of the old civilization was struggle against nature envisaged by crude and cruel competition. The ideal of competition as a valid individual, social, national and international aim, however, is being happily abandoned by our modern educators. Should it not give way to constructive and positive cooperative-competition?

How does this stress upon competition affect individual play, the wider social play status and the hygienic relationship of child and teacher? It is generally conceded that personality maladjustments may naturally develop from prolonged exposure to severe and unfair competitive relationships. Satisfaction in rewards based upon being first does not take into consideration the wide range of individual differences and allows satisfaction to but few. Inward struggles and deep emotional disturbances are created in the vain attempt of all to gain first place. Failures result in undesirable personality traits and feelings of inadequacy due to frustration. One abnormal condition creates another, and the child thus frustrated may try to compensate by extreme attempts to gain attention and through heroic and possibly theatrical efforts attempts to prove the worthwhileness of his personality. Accustomed to accept only victory, he is in no condition to receive the personal and social disapprobation of defeat. He should be conditioned to realize the inevitable and positive value of reasonable experience in defeat by objectively analyzing the factors or entering into it. At an early impressionable age, as "prototype" to use Adler's term is established bearing the inerasable impressions and sad implications of frustration and defeat.

Now what does the undiscerning child think of all this? Not being able to critically evaluate the situation he accepts it and reacts against it by many forms of evasive and compensatory behavior. The alert teacher will seek to find what the child thinks about this most significant situation. Generally it may be said that the child approaches life through play, the parent perceives life as competition, and old folks look upon life as a struggle and a rest. What can education contribute to a more effective and hygienic play psychology? We are on the threshold of a new social order of liberal and democratic methods, new ideals which may assist in a reorientation toward competitive educational practices and beliefs. The success motive in learning is decried and in words of Henry Suzzallo "the effective social person rather than a successful individual," is the objective prototype of the future. We must conceive of civilization as kindly and as training a nation of cooperative people, and the new democratic aspiration as stressing service and satisfaction, which come from social objectives rather than personal success resulting from unwholesome competition. The altruistic thrill of participation and developmental control of one's own body will replace the self-satisfactions of egotistic success in overcoming others. The larger altruistic task of sharing common tasks, problems and opportunities will replace the personal egotistic motivation. And to this end social approval rather than exclusive individual satisfaction will be provided. Human interest and sympathetic understanding of others as well as one's own biological and social needs will be an important part of the teachers' equipment and probably more fundamental than is academic and technical training.

Such a philosophy does not deny any value in competition. Individual rivalry is race-old and is inherent both in the environmental atmosphere and in the individual and is most easily aroused. A rivalry based upon cooperative striving in place of individual self-seeking may provide the more wholesome hygienic aim. Such a viewpoint would emphasize the human fellowship created in playing between human personalities for the satisfaction of all rather than the crude expression of contending forces playing as efficient automatons. The child would thus be enabled to use the many pleasurable outlets of play to get acquainted with the world he lives in. Just as he might meet with confidence a friend in whom he has a feeling of mutual understanding vitalized by previous experiences of altruistic helpfulness.

The modern teacher will see many opportunities to utilize play in teaching the child most fundamental humanitarian lessons. The aggressive qualities spontaneously developed in play may most naturally lead to unwholesome traits such as a smart bragging attitude, domineering trends and over-assumptions of individual importance. The wise teacher will seek to replace these undesirable manifestations by a preferred emphasis upon more socialized approaches such as the humility which comes from modesty rather than submissiveness. The discriminating parent will encourage power and poise which emanate from a tenderness and understanding mildness. While such unassuming qualities may afford the most lasting and substantially satisfying traits, it would indeed be most foolish to expect a child to be entirely unpretentious in play. The empowering control, however, which comes from mental poise is an aim both practical and attainable. The control of oneself before trying to control the physical elements of the game is fundamental and should be more adequately emphasized in the genetic development of the child.

In hygienic practice, play should not be viewed as a predominating display of aggressive action. The observant teacher will note that the child's behaviour is very different when he is with others from what it is when he is alone. He being a social animal may easily be stimulated to greater effort by his companions. He may most naturally make the mistake of surpassing others, the dominating motive in the social relation. While he may surpass some of his friends and thereby gain the immediate satisfaction of competitive accomplishment, he soon finds that one cannot surpass all others and may become seriously discouraged, because of his inability to do this. The realization and acceptance of failure becomes more acute than the zest of success. The superiority of cooperation over competition in hygienic practice is explained by Kirkpatrick as follows: "Cooperation involves adherence to a common plan and also individual adjustment of each to the others and thus behavior is naturally regulated more than in individual competition. The fact that a great variety of abilities may often be utilized in cooperation gives a chance for more individuals to succeed and to contribute to worthwhile ends. For these reasons co-operative activities not only prepare for citizenship, but also promote the mental health of all. They may be stimulated by common aims without engaging in contests with other groups, but are readily increased by group contests."[1]

[1] Kirkpatrick, Edwin A., "Mental Hygiene for Effective Living," D. Appleton-Century Co., 1934, p. 330.

Dr. Mandel Sherman contends that "our educational system is suffering from an overdose of success stories" and advises teachers to train their pupils to accustom themselves to failure as only a few will attain success. This viewpoint may have an important application to modern play methods. The common conception of success as consisting of preeminence in the accumulation of money or dominance in some special sphere is slowly losing ground in educational circles. The modern ideal is to establish aims upon the basis of the child's individual capacity, to have him compete against himself rather than against someone else where competition is necessary. The determination of failure or success rests upon his progress in meeting or surpassing these most natural standards. This is proving to be a sound and fundamental principle for a more hygienic approach to play. The child thus experiences a most wholesome and pleasurable expression, a growth and development by the pattern of his own individual makeup. Thus the standards set are both rational and attainable. The hygienically trained physical director or, better designated, counsellor will not destroy his capacity for distinctive service by a narrow, sordid and materialistic definition of goals which, because they exist as valid for one child, are assumed to fit into the complex pattern of another. Ideally, play should be tailor cut to fit the individual child.

The standards set for physical education if it is to reach its highest hygienic usefulness should consist of grades of activity which children of various ages can accomplish with pleasure as a result of reasonable practice. Many teachers attempting to organize or carry out a practical course of physical education for grammar school pupils will naturally question the aims as well as the physical forms of the old-fashioned conventional program. One will readily note that many children become over-resentful because of inequal situations which arise; that many emerge from the game beaten and discouraged in spirit; that others gain a false sense of winning, leading in some cases to a pert arrogance and saucy indifference to others less fortunate. Generally it appears that in proportion as many of the so-called winners are elevated by social approval the losers become depressed. The experience appears to be essentially unfair, tied down with so many conventional fetters that the fundamental expansive spirit of play is being extinguished. Many children appear to be rebuffed and thwarted as, with their inherent faith, they seek a glowing adventure in what is traditionally described as the happy play adventure.

From the viewpoint of mental hygiene it is fundamentally important to establish friendship in play. The ideal method of doing this is expressed by Cicero's fourth rule in friendship in his "Amicitia," "put yourself on the level with your friend." If the play experience is to subserve these higher aims there must be adequate opportunities for expression of individual physical, mental and social abilities. Play may be guided by one of two predominating principles —equality or dominance. Both motifs have their limitations and productive possibilities in hygienic-educational practise. Biologically speaking, no two individuals are exactly the same, therefore the fictitious quest of absolute equality of performance. Rather should each contribute according to his unique capacity for contribution to the optimum in the light of the game "stacked" for developing the best efforts of the individual or group. Equating individuals so that they may feel the stimulus of reasonable success rather than experience prolonged exposure to acts and implications of defeat is the raison d'être of the modern concept of play equality. This doctrine of *equality* is being accepted today, and is well explained by Frederick Rand Rodgers as follows: "A gang of boys choosing up sides, preparatory to a sandlot baseball game has a profound significance: it dramatizes the instinctive desire of children to play with their equals. In the absence of the third parties (coaches, spectators, reporters, parents, etc.) children and animals truly play, even in formalized combat. Not victory is their object, but the *game*. Physiologically their impulse is to exercise muscles and senses; psychologically their urge is to overcome obstacles, reasonably their desire is to seek obstacles worthy of their mettle; sociologically their impulse is to seek more and more intimate contacts with other individuals of the same species. Methodologically their procedure is to divide into opposing groups of equal numbers (pom-pom-pullaway, run-sheep-run, football, baseball); or equal skills (mumble-d-peg, marbles, tennis); or equal physical size (boxing, wrestling, football)—but always the ideal of *equality* is present in practice." [2]

The new ideal of playing merely for fun rather than to win finds ample justification in its hygienic results. The child if left to himself would lay little emphasis upon the scoring features. Then non-participants who look on and applaud the winner regardless of the equality of contestants are leading the player to over-emphasize the winning feature. From a hygienic viewpoint friendship is one of the most important contributions of the game and equality, or rather, playing to the best individual or group ability rather than dominance is an essential of friendly intercourse.

The teacher should never lose sight of the necessity of providing wisely for the social growth, interest and individualism of the child. The reapproachment of the child to social realities is best attained when he meets others in the

[2] Rogers, F. R., *Research Quarterly*, American Physical Education Association, March 1935, p. 1.

role of a non-pretentious friend. Wearing the glamorous cloak of the winner may naturally serve to further irritate those who are stinging under the lashes of defeat. The losers may pretend to admire him while actually hating him, since his high position has been attained at their expense. He has walked upon their backs to glory. The winner is envied more frequently than loved by his fellow players.

The ideal game might well result in a tie score in group contests or show individual improvement in individual play. The essence of fair play is contained only in the game in which the contestants are relatively equally matched. It is probable that the highest purpose of mental hygiene would be subserved by setting up a standard of performance in which each individual would shine to the best of his ability rather than a goal only possible of consummation by the most skillful or so low that the least skilled in the group could attain it. Kirkpatrick reminds us that nature approves individuals who are in all respects an average of the species. Yet, progress depends upon constructive deviation from the normal or average.

It is most natural that the child should feel that because he exceeds in a particular game, he excels because he outstrips, he surpasses. Many teachers unconsciously create in the child the false belief that prevalence in a game indicates predominance in other relations. A subtle impression may be likewise gained that failure in one situation may provoke failure in another. Success or failure must be understood in the light of the specific situations in which it occurred, in view of the specific factors operating at that particular time.

Some gain the impression that mere excellence in speech or skill entitles them to social preferment; such individuals should be taught that superiority in such fields does not mean they excel in all others. Improvement in any worthy avenue, however, should be encouraged. They should be stimulated to enlarge their activities into other spheres by utilizing the psychical qualities developed in play. Properly utilized, this confidence developed from play success will be a significant help in conditioning and balancing the boy or the girl with respect to the more responsible and rigorous realities of the adult made world. The queenliness which comes from culture and attainment may well beguile the imagination of the girl athlete who feels the strong urge to higher accomplishment which vigorous and successful participation develops. The child who realizes in specific situations and conditions in keeping with individual assets and liabilities opportunity for both constructive and satisfying performance is attaining a hygienic fundamental of the game. He will readily understand that it is not a disgrace to give up or retreat when the odds are unfairly against him. Because of a misunderstanding of attitude, it is with difficulty that our children are able to accept defeat with good grace.[3] Conflicts arise frequently in play because children are not conditioned to accept defeat. They are most sensitively attuned to the stimulation of winning and because of their lack of experience do not appreciate the fact that only a small number may win and that the larger number must lose. They cannot evaluate the many complex underlying conditions which determine success and failure in conventional practise. They cannot estimate the relative components determining success such as aptitudes, emotional force and stability, learning speed and capacity, constitutional and hereditary traits, training and other factors. They cannot weigh these fundamentals of interest and its relationship to effort. The activity of the child may grow to be preponderately subjective and feelings of frustration

[3] Davis, J. E., "The Utilization of Play in the Construction of Healthy Mental Attitudes," *Mental Hygiene*, January, 1936, pp. 49-54.

and inferiority result. The hygienically conscious teacher should project the lesson that rational effort will bring success but that the reward of success does not necessarily mean winning the game. The child should be impressed with the fact that losing a game well and honestly played is part of the natural uncertainties of life and is experience which should occasion no shame. The child can only learn to accept defeat gracefully and hygienically when he is taught a socially comprehensive objective for physical education.

If we are to gain the hygienic values from competition, it is necessary to group our children in accordance with their original endowments and acquired skills. Educators are getting away from the play of groups exclusively upon the basis of chronological age.

When competition in advancement is based on age, unfortunate results often accrue as the children undoubtedly resent being pitted against those of superior or inferior capacity. They may pity those of inferior endowment and be jealous of those of superior endowment. This attitude finds an unwholesome reaction in their opponents. Children, if they are afforded reasonable opportunity for success on their own and only level of ability will give little trouble. While those who are placed in situations in which they have no recourse but to display their inferiority will seek abnormal satisfactions, possibly by defiance of authority or through seeking notoriety in other anti-social channels.

Some significant changes in the child's mental health viewpoint take place when he is led to enjoy the play for its inherent values rather than the mere scoring. Little Edward, an overly stout youngster, was importuned to play ball with a dozen other children of about the same age. When it came his turn to bat, he was ill at ease because he realized he could not hit the ball as frequently and as well as the other players.

His brother perceiving this, refused to play at all. When it was explained that the idea is not to hit the ball but to play the game and that swinging and missing the ball is all right as long as one tries to hit it, the game assumed an entirely different complexion. Edward became more reassured and seemed to gain much satisfaction and was not only willing but anxious to play. Play should be viewed as a slice of life, its failures as well as successes, an expression of one's unfolding through growth and not as some severe and formal goal which, because others have reached it, exists as an unalterable obligation for each individual. Many children are rebuffed and thwarted because they are mistakenly led to feel that they must reach a certain definite standard of perfection in order to be accepted as honorable and welcome members of a play enterprise.

The relationship of competitive life to mental health is set forth by Mason and Mitchell as follows: "Competitive life is a succession of games. One who is trained in games is therefore a quicker thinker and interpreter in the midst of kaleidoscopic life of moving persons and things. The person trained in such judgments and reactions will not have identical situations facing him throughout life; but his mind will be the more adaptable for this type of experience; just as the person who has continually played at games can learn a new one easier than one who has not, and the person who has played on musical instruments can learn a new one more readily than one who has never tried such an accomplishment. This training for life need not necessarily be in athletics; the student finds much the same type of experience in serving on the school newspaper, in holding student organizations. Students who are prominent in school activities are usually prominent afterwards in their community life. The earlier training is invaluable, teaching the dangers of overconfidence and the necessity of teamwork, and giving an intimate knowledge of human nature." [4]

It is vitally important to replace the ideal of competition as a struggle against one's playmates who are conceived as enemies rather than friends. It is equally important to retain the aspect of struggle which will incite the child to improve on his own score and performance. The New Hygienic ideal emphasizes cooperative competition, satisfaction through the cooperative yet active association with others rather than the purely egotistic, restrictive and selfish aggrandizement which may so easily result from crude and cruel competition. The give-and-take attitude will provide a worthy goal for individual advancement. It will be realized that taking involves understanding as well as submissive cooperation and that giving involves a study of the needs and desires of the recipient. The new mental hygienic motif will espouse the ideal of play as a friendly cooperative spirit, a social quest, challenge, adventure, an attitude of democratic equality of "individual and group solidarity."

PLAY AS CONFLICT

The concept of play as essentially a conflict should be carefully examined by the teacher for its significant hygienic implications. One rarely finds a child who is unresponsive to play. There are many children, however, who are rebuffed by specific types of recreation and there are others who although atypical, are puzzlingly unresponsive to any type of play activity. In the absence of pathological conditions which are apparent to the medical practitioner, the unresponsive child may be passing through some mental conflict, a possible

[4] Mitchell and Mason, "The Theory of Play," A. S. Barnes & Company, Inc., 1934, p. 236.

conflict between the ideals of those who emphasize the virtues of a cooperative society and those who view life as an essential conflict for dominance. The former would have him play for the fun of the experience while the latter would teach him to play to win. The selection of methods of playing, the goals, the spirit of the play activity all present conflicting problems to the child who is in doubt as to the fundamental nature of the game. A definite and fundamental underlying principle should be taught by the physical instructor who desires to project the higher hygienic qualities and promise. The cooperative ideal in place of the overly competitive motif contains many hygienic lessons for the parent and teacher.

The mental hygienist discerns and carefully differentiates between two kinds of conflicts, normal and abnormal, or, better, conflicts which may lead to normal or to abnormal behavior. The child's conflicts developed in his play experiences may become too intense so that he gives himself over for the largest part in attempting to solve them. In this attempt, he may isolate himself from the wholesome everyday activities. He may attempt to solve the perplexing problem by thinking it out, and such attempts may lead to serious consequences. A slow and subtle introversion may result as he directs his activities inward toward self rather than outward toward reality. He may be unable to face reality without confusion and fear and may adopt devious subterfuges in evading this situation. The wise teacher will insist that the child actually do something instead of dissipating his energy and weakening his personality by simply thinking about it. Many conflicts inhere in the overly aggressive aspects of play. Much false and dangerous teaching has resulted from the idea that conflict is the dominating characteristic of all intelligent human behavior. Modern educators emphasize cooperation as the effective key note and the criterion of happy conduct particularly in play.

The hesitancies and puzzling indecisions of many children in play are more deep-seated than the immediate situation. Psychologists have called attention to the fact that the motor responses of the child are effected by many circumstances and conditions reaching back to early impressions and extending to all the complex ramifications of the home and community environment. The child soon begins to realize that many moral precepts he has been taught are at variance with the views held by other respectable people of intelligence, that his father's views are not always the beliefs of his mother, that his new teacher's ethical code is not exactly what his old teacher followed, that the law itself is not necessarily ethical, and that even the tenets of religion differ from one another and there seems to be no ultimate and universally accepted truth about many things. Of all of these different standards which one is right? he anxiously inquires. In an aggressive world, he is called upon to act and make decisions, he must do more than simply speculate. One can readily see how serious conflicts inevitably develop. The use of force in lieu of fact to sustain obedience to restrictive authoritarian doctrines further confuse him. Norman Thomas once said in my presence, "I don't object to the teacher saying 'God says so and so,' but I do object to her saying 'God and I say so and so.'"

Teachers may unconsciously contribute to the detrimental idea and ideal of play as an antagonizing encounter. The parent, however, is more susceptible to this false perspective. It is most natural for many to look upon the play of children as an aggressive adventure in which the harsh and hard qualities of dominance may find expression. We tell Jimmy to play hard, to get his man, to fight hard, to battle until the end. In this way there creeps into the play experience many qualities that we as teachers do not desire to become a part of our pupils. Unconsciously the player adds to his personality make-up displeasing tinges of uppishness, rankling traits of smart demeanor, subtle egotistic attitudes and aggravating acts of discourtesy, selfish sentiment and many other repellent traits. Some of these may well serve to set him aside from his playmates and make the attitude of others toward him more resentful than friendly. Thus, it frequently happens that these quests for dominance fostered in our children's play lead to conflicts with the very social graces we are attempting to inculcate. Thus, two great conflicting objectives, dominance and submission enter into the early play life of the child in his striving for expression. The wise utilization and coordination of these impulses present a most important problem for education. Play may assist by bringing about a harmonious balance between these forces of personality. The teacher must realize that these inflaming disharmonies are within the individual himself and that through a proper balancing of impulses, wishes, and capacity, a unity of the individual himself may be achieved. This field of the child's own nature rather than the discrepancies in the environment should be stressed. The teacher should study the field of the unconscious in its theoretical relationship and effect upon the play experiences of the child.

The attachment of father to a daughter and mother to son has been stressed in its relationship to conflicts, particularly to the "Oedipus Complex." The jealousy of the son toward his father and the daughter toward the mother often results, in accordance with the Freudian theory, in an unconscious desire of every son to kill his father and marry his mother and every daughter to kill her mother and marry her father. The sexual conflict in some cases becomes severe and persists as a damaging influence upon the unconscious level. Many cases in abnormal psychology illustrate the value of play companionship with others of the same sex in assisting the child to break away from the child-parent relationship and to identify himself in wholesome relationship with the opposite sex. The realization of sex differences tends to make the opposite sex more interesting. This interest should be wholesome and not morbid. A natural adjustment is secured as a child realizes these differences in terms of skill and capacity as developed in play. The companionship of parent playing with child may assist through the dissipation of many of these disorganizing and disintegrating jealousies.

The love fixation of the child for the mother results in an intense attachment which is both natural and normal. The child learns to love in this manner and gains the deepest sense of security and pleasure at his mother's breast. When he grows older, however, he undergoes a slow transition during which he learns to admire the father who assumes the proper role of parent. Jealousy is replaced by respect as many significant alliances are made between father and child. As they do things together, take hikes, play ball, intimate and most meaningful contacts are formed, and the qualities of manliness slowly replace infantile cravings as the child is taught to do manly things.

The young child who is growing into an understanding of more complex play activities may often develop conflicts because of fine drawn and artful taboos and regulations. Increasing complexities confuse the child and in his discouragement, he may adopt a disabling attitude of futility. This presents a characteristic situation in contemporary child's play. How can we better it? The child should be taught above all that many complex rules and regulations, and situations may never be understood by him just as all other people understand them; that while he cannot grasp all these puzzling intricacies, he can understand the broad and growing principles of loving humanism, that it is always a source of happiness to be kind and considerate. In this way he grows to be big and strong. He should be led to seek the confidence which repays the beneficent big brother attitude, and the personality poise and enrichment which such a happy principle of action so well develops. He should be taught the joy which comes from "Transforming the crowd into the community," to use Jack's socially significant phrase; the zest which comes from playing and working together for collective ends, ends which have not been weakened and distorted by selfish and restrictive individual aims. Educational methods should organize and utilize such social trends and potentialities.

Many habits of the child reflect cramping limitation and confining indecision. Immaturity of effort, imbalance between effort and result, lack of skill, all these elements entering into the gradual adjustment to the rigors of conventional living may lay the foundation for conflicts and worries. Tics and neurotic symptoms may possibly develop when these conditions are not taken into consideration. The restrictive factors may be advantageously replaced by the more spontaneous and expansive factors of suitable play presented as educational material. A child's development may easily turn, to use Adler's expression "upon either the useful or the useless side of life." A child's mind may be filled with many worries not causally related to actual experience. In evading these worries or compensating for them, pleasant fictions may creep in and resultant fantasy creations may be worse than worries, in their demoralizing effect upon the personality.

A child's life is composed largely of fantasy. The healthy boy or girl, however, progressively distinguishes between the real and the ideal and each day through growth and appreciation departs farther from the fanciful toward objective understanding and appreciation. Vicarious play may be the cause of many conflicts and worries because of uncertainty and vacillation between the real and the ideal. Little Johnny who lives in the country goes with his city cousin to see a Wild West movie show. Upon his return to the country, he engages in Wild West play himself and in a wholesome way lives in overt action, the heroic play pictures imprinted in his mind. His city cousin, however, hemmed in as he is, has no opportunity to express the play situations and urges awakened in viewing the motion picture, and may represent these experiences in fantasy and day-dreaming. Complexes develop as result of the opposed feelings which co-exist and frustrate the child.

One cause of conflict in child's play is jealousy and this trend should be carefully studied by the teacher. The uncomfortable feelings which the child shows when someone else receives more praise than he is a most natural desire of the child for recognition. He may attempt to escape from this discomfort by making an uncomplimentary remark about the favored individual or, by some devious method, attempt to praise himself. In many cases, however, the child will feel deeply depressed and may grow irritable. This painful situation frequently results from the foolish urges and lures of competition, from the deceptive idea that the only value of the game is to win or to gain some personal preference of egotistic prominence. These same jealous children placed into another situation in which all can receive satisfaction rather than an idolized few will respond in a most wholesome manner. The jealous child in play is most frequently seeking some method to gain recognition which he feels he justly deserves and play properly organized from a hygienic standpoint will allow him this salutary aggressive expression. Conflicts in play frequently produce puzzling types of behavior which clinical analysis prove to be attempts at compensation. Such compensatory behavior is well illustrated in the case of a six-year-old child who in the first year's schooling caused the teacher much trouble with his unpredictable behavior. When the children sang he invariably made facial grimaces and seemed to delight in being out of tune with the others. In his play he was overly aggressive and so rough that other children hesitated to play with him. The teacher tried various methods of dealing with him and was unsuccessful in most cases. A psychiatric examination disclosed that while he was on par with the others mentally, he was undernourished physically and for the first time in a social group he had felt the impact of others whom he realized were superior to him in physical endurance and in the social graces. He craved recognition. Upon the suggestion of the psychiatrist the teacher's approach to the emotional re-education of the child was upon the sensory level. He was made a leader in simple group games and was made to feel that he was worthwhile and a most important factor in the school program. Thus appealing to his feeling of recognition his attitude underwent an important transformation and he became more constructive in his outlook and his conduct was integrated upon a more satisfactory level.

Then, there was a ten-year-old girl who became most offensive during the play period, although she was quiet and cooperative in the other classes. She appeared at times to be disinterested and then, as if out of a clear sky, she would abuse her playmates and threaten them until she had interrupted or otherwise frustrated their play. The teacher tried many approaches to this conduct problem. Thinking the child needed encouragement and redirection into other type of play, new games were introduced for her but without avail. The psychiatrist examined the content of her emotional life and found that she had formed associations of play which were causing the trouble. At the age of five she had her first opportunity to play with others when her parents moved. The next door neighbor's children came in a crowd to play with her and she soon found herself surrounded and intimidated by many children, some older than she was. Used to being given free rein in her home, she soon realized that this old freedom of action did not work with others. Thus, the early play relationship became associated with the disjunctive emotions of fear and hatred, of restriction and dispossession. Since these conditions had been formed years ago and organized over a long period the psychiatrist realized that a comparatively extensive period of re-education must follow the interpretation of the basic cause. A period of social reorientation in the class room and in the home was necessary. The child was taught that the present attitude toward play was the result of something which had happened years ago and was no longer present. She was taught some simple play skills and allowed to play in individual relationship until she felt more at ease with others. Such conflicts inhering upon the level of the unconscious require the direction of the psychiatrist for their solution.

A twelve-year-old child presented difficulty because of his tendency to bully others in their play. He was above the average in intelligence and strong and well nourished physically. Sadistic tendencies would crop out in his play and he would try to excuse this behavior by devious rationalizations. He seemed unable to control this behavior although he appeared to be ashamed of such domineering attitudes and acts. Many approaches, including disciplinary punishments, were utilized by the teacher but to no avail. Calling attention to these aberrations seemed only to lead the boy into empty excuses. Going into the pre-school history, the psychiatrist discovered that the child had frequent difficulties with a next door playmate who was stronger and more aggressive. The next door playmate had a habit of pulling his hair and because of his tenacity and greater strength would leave him in a frenzy. One day the father, observing this, importuned his son to get even with his playmate and pull his hair in turn. The child was in a panic but due to the stern demands of his father grabbed the playmate and held on to his hair until he started to cry. After that the child had a strong impulse to hurt others and this sadistic expression most naturally came to the surface in his play. The psychiatrist realized that such firmly embedded impulses are not to be solved through an appeal to the reason of the child but must be solved through a reorientation of attitude resulting from a recognition of the emotional cause. Emotional re-education in which the capacity of the child for skills in play may act as a sublimating factor most frequently provides an effective approach. In this case, these anti-social aggressive impulses were slowly modified as the child was redirected to higher types and grades of play skills presented as hygienic education.[5]

The problem of socializing and sublimating the fight urge so easily awakened in play experiences provides a pressing responsibility upon the parent and teacher. Cannot we teach our children that the higher joys of play are inherent in constructive processes and are opposed to fighting which is fundamentally a destructive activity leading to unwise patterns of behaviour, that fighting has no more place in the

[5] Davis, J. E., "The Utilization of Play in the Construction of Healthy Mental Attitudes," *Mental Hygiene*, January, 1936, pp. 49-54.

truly educational concept of play than it has in other avenues of orderly approach to the higher values of living, that fighting involves chaos and loss in spirit and body while true playing means psychic peacefulness and orderly growth into higher levels of integration, that play assists in building desirable values both mental and physical while fighting destroys friendships and distorts other values of social living, that fighting suppresses our higher ideals while play expresses our nobler desires in wholesome and pleasurable ways. The child so sensitively attuned to the fighting aspect of play needs guidance if we are to turn him at this impressionable moment of childhood into an appreciation of the higher values of play hygienically conceived as a social rather than a severely individual and egotistic expression.

The main difficulty in realizing such a hygienic motif is due to the fact that many destructively aggressive trends of the child do not emerge in conduct as discernible examples of raw fighting. They are masked in many distortions and complicated by falsifications of disguised obeisance to our social graces. The fighting spirit is most often present as a destructive influence, however, to be discovered and redirected by the discerning counsellor.

COMPENSATION

Passive play has been viewed as a transfer of oneself into an imaginative situation as a sort of vacation from "one's everyday self and the routine of everyday living." In active play the child more nearly approaches actual living and the traits and forms of play blend into growth processes and become happily entangled in more responsible levels of living until play may slowly merge into work. In this intricate though natural adaptation, the child often substitutes fancies for realities until with growth and development these childish ideals may be transformed into adult forms of expression. It cannot wait to enjoy these cherished realities of an adult made world and employs many mechanisms of early play experiences to compensate for manifold things which are unrealized in actuality. Thus play becomes a most important vehicle for compensation. The child is, through this medium, enabled to make up in a way satisfactory to himself, although not always satisfactory to society, for many feelings of inadequacy and frustration. He identifies and reidentifies himself through play to both imaginative and actual situations. Since he cannot hit the ball well he plays that he is Babe Ruth and propels the ball in imaginary flight over the fence for a home run. The motivation which such reverie provides is a most necessary psychological momentum to spur him on to further growth and progress.

Destructive feelings of inadequacy are most frequently awakened and sustained, however, by a foolish emphasis upon the all importance of winning. Our social and economic structure has emphasized the ideal of competition rather than cooperation and in many educational relationships, including recreation, the distorting imprint of this philosophy has led to harmful reaction. The child tries to compensate in his play for his inability to attain the ideals of such a false viewpoint. He becomes impressed with might and power; dynamic situations, predominating people and potency as shown in nature and man-made things enrapture him. Cyclopean monsters, Spartan fortitude, hardy pioneers, heroic stories— all contain the element of magnitude and moving power vitalized and attuned to his imagination. Overpowering one's fellows, violent or even brutal acts bring exciting pleasure. The integration of a more social-individual relationship provides a fundamental objective for progressive education.

There are many indirect compensations from play. I was impressed by a boyfriend who, although but ten years of age, was an unusually adept baseball player. His happy demeanor was especially evident in the game and his emotional responses seemed so notably wholesome and well balanced. When I casually asked him why he liked baseball, the answer was most interesting. He stated in substance that at first he did not like the game because at the age of six, he hurt his hand while catching the hard ball and after that discontinued the game for some years. Then his brother became sick and my friend became much worried about his condition, but the crisis passed and the brother began to get better. One of his first diversions during the convalescent period was to throw a baseball. Feeling that he was assisting in his brother's improvement, the boy played ball with him and noted with deep gratification his eventual recovery. These significant early associations invested the play experience between the brothers with a deep and satisfying feeling. My friend was most impressionable and subject to deep moods of depression. At such times he confided that he found nothing so pleasantly stimulating and devoid of worries as a baseball practice between his brother and himself.

Every boy and girl seeks to enhance or add to his prestige. Feelings of inability to get along or to keep up with the crowd lead to many disorganizing conflicts. Many of these individuals can be assisted to make a satisfactory adjustment if some single trait can be found which will enable them to show superiority toward others; for this distinct purpose, hobbies and other forms of recreation may have hygienic value. Conflicts of insecurity may be overcome and greater social recognition may result from thus utilizing the sensory level upon which to construct higher mental attitudes. Many sensitive children are not conditioned to accept failure or to acknowledge inability. As their attention is injudiciously called to their inferiority, they will make a great and at times heroic effort to excel in these traits in which they have but little or no ability. The guidance of the teachers in these cases can turn personality defeat into personality success by finding traits in which the individual excels and assisting him to develop these traits as compensation for those in which he is deficient.

Many children are unable to sublimate their feelings of failure in unwisely chosen and directed play activities and one of the most common reactions in this case is for the child to project his defects upon someone else. While he acknowledges that he cannot play baseball, he observes somewhat complacently that he is not so bad after all and that Willie is much worse than he is, and he may go further and blame others for the defects in his play. The reason he could not catch the ball was because Willie threw it too high or too hard. He may become most critical of the play of others in an unconscious attempt to hide his own poor playing. The unsuccessful player may attempt to compensate also by identifying himself with another individual who is especially skillful or with a team, the united action of which will hide his defect and the success of which will increase his prestige. He refers positively to the successful players as we. These identifications are, of course, important molds of adjustment and may also lead to desirable behavior as when the individual identifies himself with some worthwhile social cause. Higher levels of compensation should always be sought. Edwin, a toddler of 18 months, insisted on stripping the family garden of its blossoms. Each time they saw him near the flowers, the father or mother would go to him, hold the flower gently and smell it—then they allowed him to smell it too; each time exclaiming over the flower's fragrance. So they eliminated the habit of picking by substituting the habit of smelling.

One of the undesirable compensations attempted in play experiences is unwholesome criticism. Many children who feel their weaknesses most keenly may attempt to cover up their own deficiencies by critical gossip. Although they do not realize it, it is not so much to present a true picture of the foibles and weaknesses of others as it is to divert attention from their own inferiority. Many children attempt also to criticize themselves feeling that they are thus in position to receive praise from others.

It should not be inferred from this that the child may not gain many satisfying and wholesome compensations from the adult made world in play. The child desires to do mannish things; he cannot manipulate an aeroplane, but he can propel a ball through the air and in many other forms of play action can demonstrate a growing capacity to do more mature things, thus forming many wholesome compensations which may spur him on to do things which the adult deems worthwhile.

The child is constantly seeking to break away from the restrictions imposed by an adult made world. The rigid uniformity and unbending regularity of many processes in the home and in society are repugnant to the immature and growing child. A little boy when asked why he preferred to leave his warmly heated home to play outside in winter weather, answered, "I can put my things where I want to when I play outside, but I have to put them where you want me to when I am at home." Many of the compensations in play are felt rather than understood by the child. A rich symbolism in play and much mysticism provide the expansive play spirit. As the child develops, he utilizes an increasing number of symbols and as the environment becomes more intricate, they take on many associations and in turn become more complex. The child's thought becomes enriched through symbolism and instead of thinking entirely of tangible objects, he may think of something which has attached itself to that object. Thus the mechanism of play becomes surrounded by an aura of entrancing mystery of many things subtly felt rather than definitely understood.

One of the finest compensations of play is a "saving sense of humor." One of the best ways to meet and correct an oversevere emphasis upon the necessity of winning which may lead to a disintegrating fear of losing, is to meet the situation through some humorously relaxing approach. The teacher above all should have a hardy sense of humor; with this attribute he will be able to present play as a bright and happy rather than a serious and overly responsible activity. Such laughter and fun make up the relaxing phase of recreation which is a natural complement to the severe striving. The ideal experience is a dual one, a rhythm of severe concentration followed by a relaxing, light, and restful phase.

Compensation as manifested in play may take two forms; an attempt based upon feelings of inferiority to attain prestige in some other way or an attempt also based upon feelings of inferiority to develop and increase the capacities in which he is knowingly and plainly deficient. In the former case, the sense of inadequacy may spur the child on to worthwhile accomplishment. In the latter case, however, there is frequently a failure to see things in their proper perspective, leading to "unprofitable discontent, feelings of incongruity and disproportion" to use Adolf Meyer's terminology. The small child most naturally attempts to do big things in the game and his compensatory attempts may lead to peculiarities in conduct with rationalizations for each failure and even refusal to accept defeat. The informed teacher will readily detect these destructive as well as wholesome methods of compensation. In games, many such harmful compensatory attempts may be adequately understood and met by the teacher who studies them from the levels of the child's maturity and development. Immaturity of physical and emotional growth will explain many individual attempts to attract attention for the purpose of proving the worthwhileness of their pattern of behaviour. The little boy who retired from the game of baseball rebuffed because he could not hit the ball presented a problem more in the sphere of mental hygiene than physical education. The teacher schooled in hygienic practise realized that he would be able to hit the ball as he grew older and his skill developed. He inducted him into the less complex activities of throwing and then catching the ball. This form of compensation based upon the realization of the increasing control which comes with age and growth processes is one of the most valuable psychic contributions which play may make to the armamentarium of mental hygiene.

FANCIFUL AND REAL LIVING

We must think of the child in some such dynamic way as this; thinking of it as thrust into the world full of potentialities which can only come into being tried out in innumerable directions. Just as the searchlight penetrates the gloom as its rays move first in this direction then in that, so the child by its constant activities, the result of its varied and shifting interests, lights its way into the highways and byways of reality.—WILLIAM A. WHITE.[6]

[6] White, W. A., "The Mental Hygiene of Childhood," Little, Brown and Company, 1905, p. 88.

Parents and teachers alike may be inclined to look upon the child's daydreams as unnatural and therefore undesirable. Because of this attitude many children do not disclose their imaginative activities directly. These phantasies, however, must find some overt expression and the child ordinarily satisfies himself in make-believe play. As he becomes older, this expression through phantasy becomes more difficult because of the restrictions and inhibitions imposed by adult conventions. Two types of daydreaming develop; the natural and casual daydreaming which is soon over and the more systematized phantasy which grows into a continuous story resulting in a repetition of the same daydreaming pattern.

It is generally recognized today that casual phantasy thinking is a normal mode of growth and expression. The systematized phantasy which may lead to harmful mental conflicts often occurs because the child cannot attain satisfaction through more realistic approaches. If taught that he cannot gain every desire and must accept frequent failures as well as successes he may not be so liable to resort to excessive or abnormal daydreaming. The coach who overemphasizes the necessity of winning the game may unwittingly drive the child to excessive imaginative activity. Spurred on by the coach, he forms a strong desire to win and cannot be unconcerned when he loses. Overly sensitive and conscientious types may as a compensation for these frustrations retreat into a wish fulfilling world of unreality. It is, therefore, most important for those in charge of physical education to set up standards for winning which are attainable with a reasonable amount of effort for the individuals or groups concerned. They should be careful to differentiate aims for various types as well. It is also very important to enter sympathetically into the make-believe play of the child. The most alert and intelligent children may develop a very rich world of phantasy creation and associates should accept this projection of the child's interest as a natural evolution of growth.

Harmful effects of phantasy may result when for some reason the particular play activity loses interest or when diverse aims bring about confusion. It is most important to project play as a simple, noncomplicated activity; once it becomes overly complex, the inherent zest which James ascribes to its automatic nature becomes lost and the child may retreat into a more pleasant field of phantasy.

C. H. Green [7] describes four types of phantasy: (a) "display phantasy illustrated by the dreamer who performs a feat which brings him applause; (b) saving phantasy in which the dreamer performs some act really beyond his capacity, allowing him to gain the devotion and applause of the rescued person; (c) phantasy of grandeur in which the daydreamer becomes a member of royalty or some deity; (d) phantasy of homage, the daydreamer accomplishes some unusual feat for one of his admirers."

These types of phantasy are well illustrated in the play life of the child. Little Johnny comes home from a baseball game where he sees adults play. In a daydream just before falling to sleep, he knocks a home run and hears the large group of spectators applauding him. Little Willie is a hero worshipper; he hears people discuss the heroic act of the young man who rescued a drowning person. He does not know how to swim but in his daydreams he performs the heroic act of rescuing a drowning person and thus gains the praise and approbation of others. Mary gains many satisfactions in being transported through daydreams into the personage of royalty in make-believe play; she becomes a

[7] Green, C. H., "Psychoanalysis in the Classroom," G. P. Putnam's Sons, 1922, pp. 42-43.

queen to whom others must render homage or a deity whose pronouncements are final.

Most children in their play experiences change their phantasies. Little Mary may become a queen one day in her play and the next day a domestic servant; one day she may have all power and the next day be overcome by her enemies. In the play experiences the child may utilize as part of his phantasy development traits which appear to assist him gain satisfaction through success. If these imaginary creations are successful, he may continue to use them and may develop them into systematized phantasy and if this self-created world is more satisfying, he may unduly neglect the world of reality and develop into an unwholesomely introverted child.

An interesting psychological mechanism frequently presents itself in the child's play. The daydreamer has some desires which he cannot fulfill in reality, and, therefore, seeks through phantasy. He may project upon others the experience which he would like to have himself and thus attain a vicarious satisfaction. This type of conduct is characteristically evasive and it is harmful to hygienic conduct. The young child has in most cases a very normal expression through phantasy, there being very little symbolic behavior noted at this period. The difficulties arise later with the imposition of restrictions and taboos by adult conventionality. This phantasy expression becomes restricted. At this point, the guidance of the teacher is most important in retaining the vitalizing force of symbolic behavior while at the same time soundly aligning it with the demands of healthful reality.

One of the best illustrations of an abnormal emphasis upon the utilization of phantasy is afforded in examining the play of the deeply introverted psychotic individual. Receiving his deepest satisfactions from subjective rather than external creations, this puzzling individual gradually buttons himself up in an increasingly complex phantasy world, many events of his experience becoming cloaked in symbolism. In his play, he will repeat many of the early pleasurable childhood patterns and while the acts which have become automatic are carried out in many cases with precision there are added many incongruous gestures and movements which serve to satisfy far-fetched symbolic representations.

The effect of phantasy upon play depends upon whether the creations are casual or are more severe systematic forms. In the former case, the child may be momentarily diverted but his attention can easily be regained. These diversions probably rest the child and make his activity more interesting because of this change. The systematic phantasies interfere with the normal action of the game and have a detrimental effect; generally the child weakens his customary effort, his concentration lags and he may not be able to make satisfactorily the plays which he has accomplished previously in a faultless manner. He may carry out certain automatic features of the game while his active attention is occupied entirely with his phantasy. Or, in situations requiring voluntary attention and awareness, he may be unable to carry out the desired act because of his absorption in phantasy. He may evade the situation by pretending to concentrate upon the game while he is actually preoccupied in phantasy.

While in some cases the child gives verbal expression to his phantasy, he does this rarely in his play experiences. Other children make fun of him as soon as he attempts to talk out loud in these daydreams. When playing by himself, however, he may resort to this expression of phantasy. The teacher or parent who finds the young child talking to himself in his play should ordinarily encourage him and in that way give him the confidence which comes from understanding that it is normal to daydream and that he need not hide it. Can play have any efficacy in overcoming excessive phantasy preoccupation? Educators are calling attention to the potency of indirect rather than direct methods of modifying behavior. To tell the young child to pay attention to the game and not dream is educationally unsound. The teacher should not only allow him to express in overt action these imaginative reveries but should encourage him to find suitable forms of make-believe play for this purpose. We must realize that the excessive and systematized daydreaming of the child may be the result of an effort to compensate for some conflict. Rigid and unflinching regulations of certain forms of play may easily result in these conflicts and this fact should impress those responsible for the direction of children's play with the importance of projecting it as an inherently expansive rather than restrictive activity. Cases have been presented in which sex phantasies have been more easily resolved by heterosexual relations in play.

Excessive daydreaming invariably results in an introverted type of behavior. The individual desires to be alone and at times begins to blame himself for being alone. He makes most significant differentiations between himself and others and gradually gets away from social contacts. In this situation the socializing value of play might well be emphasized; these individuals should be progressed from individual to more social types of play in which the emphasis is placed upon concerted action and the satisfaction results from the thrill of uniting one's efforts with those of the group and thus identifying one's self with the larger and more significant task. They should be encouraged to seek satisfaction in social relationships, to find pleasurable interest in others.

The child's adjustment to real objects should be carefully guided, especially in the period from three to six years of age. Toys especially should be carefully selected so that the real world of objects will be a pleasurable one and the world of images is not the more pleasing. At this period a child may easily fall back upon fanciful creations because his actual physical environment is too complex or, as is the case with wrongly selected toys, the real objects give him pain rather than pleasure. It is most important at this formative period to keep the child from falling back upon fanciful creations.

"Play is the beginning of knowledge," says Dorsey.[8] *"Banging the rattle on the crib or getting a toe in one's mouth is an early lesson in wisdom which means there is no sharp line between playing Jesse James and being Jesse James. But the child who stops with a stick for a gun will bring down no greater game in later years than he can kill in a daydream because those of us who live only in hopes, build only castles in our own air."*

The teacher who can cultivate a well directed and rich imagination places herself upon the level of the child and is more able to interest and guide him happily. Such a resourceful counselor may change many conventional games to fit the present demands of the child. Myers calls attention to "the child who in his fourth year accomplishes things with glee when his mother suggested another character doing it, not his own person; when he was asked directly to do this he became resistive, while for instance, he refused to go to bed, he welcomed being a pig put into a pen. Another child at the age of four did not want to go to bed, his mother pretended that he was an engine and a jerk and choo-choo

---

[8] Dorsey, George A., "Why We Behave Like Human Beings," Harper and Bros., 1935, p. 355.

started him in the happiest spirits to bed." In young children, these imaginative approaches are very effective.

One of the best approaches to the problem of phantasy creation in the young child is through games associated with dressing-up. Sophie Yarnold cites some effective methods: "In the first place, this dressing-up should be for fun. The children are given picturesque ornaments and are encouraged to dress-up and make a game of it. The parent makes up the audience and insists the children put on a good show and work seriously in doing so."[9] The writer believes that the "dress-up can become one of the most interesting and useful forms of a child's play; in the first place, it has a great merit of appealing to children universally as being great fun. From the time they are little they love to put on something which has nothing to do with their own everyday clothes. It may be grotesque and picturesque, it doesn't matter. What is important to the children is that they are no longer Bobby and Alice but become new and uninhibited persons who can live according to the dictates of their own imaginations."

In this way they make up their own little place; they first begin by putting on a large hat or coat asserting that they are big and then they aspire not only to look like but to act like someone else. Creative urge may be activated as the boys and girls attempt to make different costumes. Girls can be taught to sew more easily and the boys may set up scenery for troupes; when the show is all lined up they may charge a small admission.

While this form of play has excellent possibilities in a more happy and healthful adjustment to reality, there is one pitfall which Miss Yarnold states should be avoided with children. The ill adjusted child who dresses up to compensate for a sense of inadequacy or failure in actual life may seek

[9] Yarnold, Sophie, "The World A Stage," *Hygeia*, March, 1935.

through this game some heroic role which would compensate for this failure. He may want to dress like a soldier, a football player, or a sea captain and may want to wear these costumes not only for play but all day. His dressing-up represents more reality to him than the actualities of his everyday existence. In this case Miss Yarnold sought "for his sense of insecurity." She "casually laughed off, as being beneath his dignity, his tendency to feel big because of his clothes and pointed out to him that his method of having a sense of achievement lacked integrity and treated it as rather childish. It took him some time to know the difference between two forms of dressing-up but once he acknowledged them to himself, this wasteful type of fanciful life was superseded by an honest and useful one."

In developing the proper utilization of phantasy, parents should aim at the development of wholesome aggressive traits. They should guide their children into progression, from states of dependence to independence, from tagging at mother's skirts and heartstrings to seeking other things and other interests. Play as it contributes to this emancipation from the solicitous atmosphere of the home love to aggressive interests in outside spheres will assist in replacing phantasy by reality.

It is most important for the teacher to inquire into and to study the underlying reasons for the child selecting certain types of play or emphasizing unduly certain episodes or situations. Play may satisfy the phantasy creation of the child, build up abnormal values to compensate for deficiencies, mistakes and failures. William A. White calls attention to this sort of play in some children who, realizing that their parents are not the all-sufficient and all-powerful characters they thought them to be, create in play phantasy new all-important and all-powerful individuals to fictitiously represent them or to take their place.

THE TIMID CHILD

The overcautious, hesitant, and uneasy child presents a serious problem in mental health adjustment. Teachers and parents as well are prone to overemphasize behavior maladjustments of the active and aggressive child, and assume somewhat complacently that the quiet submissive individual shows satisfactory mental adjustment. Psychiatrists are calling attention to the important fact that the submissive rather than the aggressive individual presents the greater threat to mental health. It is very important for educators to replace feelings and habits of fear with understanding so that an adjustment may be obtained upon a higher and more healthful level of security. There is probably no more natural means of awakening aggressive qualities in the timid child than through play which is carefully conditioned to his mental and physical capacity and interest. Fact gained from sensory experience in play may prove an antidote for some fears. The child should be taught that many of the things which he fears have little or no objective reality, or are associated with things which have caused fears in the past, but are no longer present. A recognition of the emotional cause may assist in dissipating the fear. As the child grows, in active experience, many of these fears are desensitized and cast aside as idle phantasies.

There are, however, many fears which the child cannot so easily dispel. An imaginative little boy of nine told me that he had many worries about the world. He felt that the sky might fall in, the sun might crumble and fall on him; he had fears of kidnappers, robbers, et cetera. When asked of what fears he had in games he played, he replied that he had none, except for the bruises he got from football. It is a noteworthy fact that children placed in a proper play environment develop few if any fears. Some fears arising from the physical elements of play can be dissipated by methods of direct approach. For example, the child who was afraid of the water was allowed to put sticks and play boats in the water before efforts were made to get him into the bathtub; in this manner, he soon became used to the water and enjoyed paddling and other forms of water playing.

Parents are accustomed to feel that the sense of security can be most naturally awakened and best sustained in the family environment. White has taught us that many threats to wholesome personality inhere in the family relationship. Educators, however, have discovered that a hygienic sense of security can be obtained in group relationships typified in play. The experience of other countries has shown that a child may be taught to find security in the group as well as in the family.

Caroline B. Zachry says, "In Russia, for instance, emphasis is on the group. We see shock brigades of little children. We are disturbed by the uprooting of family life. An attempt is being made to give to young children a sense of security based on something different from all that we have known in the past. In the past and in our country today, a sense of security still comes from the family, but in Russia it comes from the group." [10]

Observant parents often utilize play to dissipate unwholesome fears. One mother reports that when her son was three, he developed a fear of the dark and using the old-fashioned game of hide-and-seek, she at last established a cure. Father

[10] Zachry, Caroline B., *Child Study Magazine*, April, 1934.

would hide behind some piece of furniture in some darkened room, mother would try to find him. Mother took the next turn to hide; the next step was to take Sonny with them when they hid. The next and final step was to persuade Sonny to hide in the darkened room alone. This progressive readaptation effected the cure. He was next sent to turn on lights and never would he mention that he was afraid of the dark. At the age of six, the mother reports that he doesn't know that he was afraid of the dark. Another approach was followed in the case of John, who at the age of four created a fear of lightning and whenever a storm came up his parents tried to bring this fear out into the open and attacked it directly. With each roll of thunder, the mother cried out "Booh! Boom!" and encouraged him to make the noise, trying to outdo the thunder. This doing outlet for the emotion of fear gave him a new direction and he began to change to an active enjoyment of the storm.

It is well to understand that fears may be laid down into a habit pattern. Almost all fears are learned and can be unlearned as well. John Watson has shown that there are but two unlearned fears: 1, the fear of loud sound; 2, fear of withdrawal of support. These are natural fears which are born with the child. Now what is the effect of play upon fear? Your little boy plays baseball, the hard ball is thrown past him as fast as the strong youngster can heave it; it barely misses his nose as it whizzes by. Is the boy afraid, does he fear the possibility of a broken nose? The ball is hit and your boy scrambles after it. Is he afraid the ball will take a bad bounce and hit him in the face? His playmate hits the ball and its direction is deflected, just missing him. Hundreds of times he meets situations fraught with the possibility of harm to his person while playing. He meets them adequately while thinking of making the play and realizing the emotional satisfaction and zest which comes from big muscle activity. He continues this extraverting experience without thinking of being afraid, an essentially introverting experience. This is not a counter attitude created to offset the feeling of fear which is actually present, but there is a real absence of fear in such play situations. This does not deny the fact that some children in play show fear. Fears are so very infectious and these children who have unnatural fear in play often acquire them from parents, teachers or playmates. Fears may be engendered in play unwisely selected, which requires children to do things for which they are physically or temperamentally unfit or unprepared. Such a form of fear is set up as a result of false ideals of the all importance of winning. Such a motif sets up standards of achievement which the child may not be able to attain and results in a subtle and at times paralyzing fear that he will not be a success.

Why do some children shrink from group games, develop tension attitudes, and play with indecision, hesitancy, and lack of poise? Oftentimes because the experience attempts to exact unattainable demands. Feeling that they cannot make good, they at once make rationalizing excuses for failure. It is a most common mistake of both parents and teachers, but particularly the former, to decide upon the form of the play experience first and attempt to fit the child into the required physical mold and mental sphere afterward. A natural reaction to this is loss of confidence and dodging behavior. It frequently happens that a child has a fear of meeting people in the game because of some association of an individual or individuals who have been unappreciative of his capacity and have probably ridiculed him in some early play experience. This is a very serious situation from the standpoint of mental hygiene. A child's adjustment to people is one of the most important of all the synchronizations which the game provides.

The counselor in play can be of most significant assistance to the fearful and timid child. For this individual the play should be projected as a medium for the realization of a sense of security and educational methods should be selected and directed toward the satisfaction of this fundamental need. It is of course necessary, in this objective, to shape the play to the distinctive skill capacity level of the child, but more important to select the play activity and teach it in its proper application to his personality makeup and needs.

As in all personality types, the teaching methods are of fundamental importance. The instruction should be positive rather than negative so as to assist in building up a constructively aggressive capacity. The instructor, overly anxious to assist the child, may fall into the mistaken practice of emphasizing his mistakes, of telling him not to do this or that. In this way, the child may form in his mind a prevailing picture of his mistakes which will inhibit desirable positive traits and hinder smooth and uninterrupted motor play forms, thus adversely affecting him both physically and psychically. The mental picture of the wrong way gains the ascendency in motivating and circumscribing conduct.

Upon the other hand, if the emphasis is placed upon the right way, by continually picturing right form and calling attention to the acts which are accomplished properly, the child gains confidence and comes to look upon his play experiences as happy developmental living. He gains the morale which comes from anticipating success rather than failure. His recreation becomes a most significant form of attitudinal education, inspiriting him to adjust to more responsible activities.

Some children are considered timid in play who in the

most comprehensive meaning of the term are not timid at all. Many such retiring types are simply different from their more aggressive companions. They do not like rough play such as football but are more at home in types of activity in which there is not the rough personal contact such as swimming. These children while basically different are not abnormal in the sense of being mentally ill. They should be accepted as they are and led to feel secure in the understanding that their pattern of play and life is valid and worthwhile. The psychiatrist will, of course, make a distinction between the child who is evasive and retiring from all types of play from the child who simply does not prefer the rougher types of competition. The former will be studied by the psychiatrist as possibly presenting a problem for mental hygiene.

PLAY EMBERS

Education today is emphasizing the interest of the child as the most fundamental starting point for learning. Those who are seriously concerned with play can understand it only when they realize the interest which this form of activity awakens and which in turn sustains it. Mason and Mitchell believe that "most of the organized play forms are related to the interests connected with the wishes for new experiences, security response and aesthetic enjoyment. The wishes for recognition and participation are connected with all play forms as a motivating force rather than being limited to certain patterns for their expression." [11]

The analytical student of play realizes that the interests which attach themselves to definite expression or play pat-

[11] Mitchell, E., and Mason, B., "The Theory of Play," A. S. Barnes and Company, 1934, p. 133.

terns may represent many complicated strivings and goals remote as well as near, many yearnings even independent of experience and only explainable if one could go back to racial beginning and understand the hormic plan of life.

In early youth the desires for new experience and recognition probably predominate. The aim of the teacher should be to direct the child from the over-development of such egotistic desires, while satisfying the wish for wholesome recognition. An understanding and appreciation of social values, the satisfaction which comes from higher types of social conduct should provide the aim. Mistakes are often made in this direction in making the child feel that the score is all important. The little acts of kindness, of mutual helpfulness, emotional control, sublimation and disciplined aggression are most important from a hygienic standpoint. Commendation should be provided for advancement in the social graces as well as for success as typified in attaining the highest score.

Play may teach a more hygienic approach to psychic as well as physical pain. Burnham[12] informs us that "apparently any very strong sensation whatever is painful, at least as long as mental integration and the functioning of the cortex are not involved. But as soon as the cortex functions in correlation with the higher and finer discrimination of sensations, the pain subsides. Perhaps a not uncommon experience in reading, especially if eyes are sensitive will make this clearer. If one attempts to read fine print in a poorly lighted room, at first one is likely to feel discomfort and strain or perhaps distinct pain of the eyes, but if the subject matter is extremely interesting as one goes on and becomes absorbed in the reading, the pain disappears. The higher functioning of the cortex

[12] Burnham, William H., "The Wholesome Personality," D. Appleton-Century Company, 1932, pp. 261-2.

correlating with the interest in the reading inhibits whatever discomfort and pain came from the thalamus in the beginning."

The integration which comes from properly conditioned play may assist in the training of the child toward pain and other forms of discomfort. Play may create the intense interest which, in correlation with the higher functioning of the cortex, may condition the child to accept distress in a more hygienic and wholesome manner. Psychic pain and discomfort is probably more frequent and more damaging to the well balanced personality than physical suffering and its alleviation is best effected by indirect methods, by building up a healthy functioning of the entire mental and physical organism.

A basic difference between hygienic and uncritical or undifferentiated play is that the former is based upon the interest field of the player while the latter is based upon his skill level. The former represents a primary mental experience while the latter is preponderately physical. Those who are not hygienically conscious may most naturally select players for a particular game upon the exclusive basis of their skill level and direct the activity as a physical experience. While the game cannot be divested of its inherent skill nature, the higher values of the experience will only be realized when the player is viewed as a unity moving in response to strong basic interests. This life goal determines the interests of the player and the skill aspect is simply one of the important elements in the experience. The play of the child represents a most colorful mosaic of many contributions which progress from the sensory to the mental level.

In practical application, the teacher will look for the happy emotions of the player as he tries in the game and emphasize these conjunctive elements rather than the skillful plays he makes. While we cannot divorce skill from the game, we will seek to place him in such a play situation that the personality will express itself upon a level of wholesome integration. These mental hygienic considerations are basic and of much more importance than the physical elements of good motor performance.

ENTERING A POSITIVE WORLD

If you want to see a lordly assertiveness on parade, look at the child showing off in play. One who pays more than casual attention to the most interesting phenomena of play will note that there is in addition to this aggressive type of conduct, the submissive as well. Children generally will seek new and exhilarating experiences in play. They will show a most persist aggressive tendency to get acquainted with the world in their play activities.

Robert Maynard Hutchinsons tells us, "it has never been possible to insulate young people from the world, their parents should not be unwilling to have them enter the world of ideas." There is much happy wandering into freedom as the child enters into natural play.

Psychologists are now generally agreed that the most important of the instincts from a social standpoint are those of self-assertion, the herd instinct, and the sex instinct. Self-assertion enables the individual to grow and conquer his environment, the herd instinct enables the individual to live with others and thus accomplish a unified task, and the sex instinct enables the individual to perpetuate his kind. These impulses also enable one to develop from an egocentric to a more altruistic level and are of fundamental importance for proper social as well as economic advancement.

Many teachers are much concerned about the behavior

of those who tend to disorganize the discipline of the playground. The quiet and submissive do not excite problems of discipline and are, therefore, frequently mistakenly approved and encouraged by the teacher. The evasive, daydreaming types should receive careful attention as probably needing mental health guidance. Measures should be taken to develop habits of initiative, confidence, and disciplined aggression and normal play is replete with many opportunities for such direction. The child's skill level should be determined and upon this basis, the activity should be organized so as to allow the increased satisfaction which comes from improvement in motor skills. Confidence may be most naturally and effectively aroused, and habits of evasiveness based upon feelings of inferiority may be in this manner replaced by habits of positive health awakened and organized through feelings of ability.

The teacher must know the home environment of the child if he is to understand his play interests, trends and capacity. The child's play patterns reflect the home environment and many aggressive qualities of unwholesome nature result from home surroundings. Children brought up under the misdirected control of a so-called intense Americanism, who are unconsciously bred to battle reflect in their play these unnatural aggressive qualities frequently resulting in arguments, quarrels and fights, and further resultant emotional conflicts and personality disintegration. The father who informs his wife in authoritarian tones, that he will go through fire and water to wrest a competitive business from Smith and Jones, can hardly wonder that his son will fight his way, if necessary to play first base on the local baseball team and will follow this domineering path in more responsible social relations. It is surprising how clearly and intensely the social adaptive qualities of the child are brought to light while playing. One boy whom I had known for a number of years and whom I had considered from frequent observations of his ordinary daily relations to have a fair capacity for acceptable social adjustments, proved in an informal baseball game to have a most anti-social character showing a marked inability to become a sympathetic and co-operative participant in the play relationship. Always adopting a hypercritical superior and self-sufficient attitude towards his playmates, they in turn, almost as a unit repulsed his anti-social behavior and by a most natural process cast him further away from the social group.

Sports liked best by boys between the ages of five and eight are ball games and I believe this fact illustrates the force of the aggressive qualities in play. In ball games, the boy has something to throw and to catch and these features of ball games satisfy the requirements of this aggressive impulse. The aggressive quality of the play experience may become too prominent and provide an abnormal reaction to the play situation. I remember quite vividly the reaction of a patient suffering from mental illness. In a baseball game this patient tagged a runner with most vicious zest and exclaimed, "You are out, now get the hell out of here."

However, wholesome aggressive qualities may most naturally awaken in suitable play. In a game of baseball, for example, every player feels that he can have his say. Witness the baseball chatter, the aggressive coaching, the frank expostulations, the honest criticism and zealous perception of critical situations as the game becomes more hotly contested. This is the environment par-excellence for the development of its expansive outlets so in keeping with the dynamic growth of the child. A timid little fellow who came to our community told me that he knew most of the boys although he had been here but a short while. I asked him how he became so easily acquainted. He answered significantly that all the boys went to the playground and he met them there. A patient suffering from mental illness sent me a postcard of a Y.M.C.A. where he plays handball regularly. He was a very seclusive introverted individual and could only with the greatest of effort make friendly social contacts. Having learned to play handball in the hospital, he found this medium a most valuable help in meeting strangers in the city where he lived on discharge from the hospital. The ability to play this game well gave him a sense of confidence and worthwhileness and was a most important factor in his successful social readjustment.

In some cases, we may see in the child's play, a sort of pseudo-aggressiveness, a sort of skirmishing demeanor, which results from a sense of fear. A boy playing baseball makes a most awkward gesture and falls down in going after the ball. His playmates make comments of ridicule and an unthinking spectator may possibly exchange glances reflecting a feeling of pity or even derision. Such taunts are most harmful and may cause the boy to adopt a feigned and unnatural aggressiveness resulting from feelings of disapproval. The boy may adopt evasive tactics, he may not easily decide whether he desires to play or not, and may retire from the game at the slightest provocation. From this seemingly insignificant experience, attitudes and feelings of inadequacy and inferiority may develop and prove a disturbing factor to the development of a necessary sense of confidence and positiveness in later life.

The child enters an adult-made world, a world which threatens his individual unity; he feels many times that his rights are not guaranteed. He seeks an approach to adult responsibilities which he can understand and which at his level is attainable and may be motivated by pleasurable emotion. The wise parent and teacher will satisfy this elemental need by assisting the child to develop motor skills. Such development will lay the basis for the development of most fundamental psychic qualities. The happiest experiences of the child are associated with the development of skills as reflected in control over its own body and increasing control of its environment. The close relationship of such physical adjustment to mental health has been inadequately stressed by both educator and psychiatrist. Experience amply confirms the belief that such growth in motor adaptation to reality creates a sense of wholesome self-realization, of personal worthwhileness. These feelings of adequacy breed confidence and lead to the development of a more tolerant attitude towards others and are helpful adjuncts to happy socialization. Self-respect is a psychic requisite to satisfactory group adjustment. The child must be understood as a skill hungry animal and this primitive urge affords a most fundamental basis for educational practises and methods of high hygienic import.

PLAY OF THE MENTALLY WELL AND MENTALLY ILL

Since the mentally disordered individual has been raised to the dignity of a sufferer of disease and the subject of mental treatment has been approached through more dispassionate and scientific methods, the parent and teacher have begun to become increasingly concerned with one of the greatest social as well as hygienic problems of our day. There is much for teachers to be concerned about in this situation. When the teacher considers that more beds are occupied in hospitals for mental disorders and mental defects than for all other forms of sickness combined, he naturally thinks of the mental stability and mental health of his own pupils.

Unfortunately, there is panacea for this profound alternation of personality which Stanley Hall calls "nature's cruel experiment." Hall goes on to remind us that it is through "this experiment" that we are able to understand much of the normal as well as abnormal functioning of the mind. Mental illness in its many forms and masques presents a problem for psychiatric study and procedure. What the teacher is interested in, insofar as play is concerned, is its possible role in a rational hygienic program.

There are two main forms of mental illness, organic and functional. It is, of course, absurd to assume that physical exercise or physical therapy can replace or repair a lesion in the brain. There is, however, much evidence upon which to base the assumption that hygienic play may promote healthful attitudes and emotional associations which may assist in a better readjustment to psychogenic disorders as well as to provide a soothing palliative for those suffering from such forms of functional disease.

As far as mental health is concerned, however, the chief contribution which physical education can give is to establish hygienic play acts and attitudes in early childhood so as to assist the individual to unfold his natural social expression in zestful and acceptible activity. "Play," says Timme, "is training in socialization." "It is by far the best and perhaps the only means of socializing the child . . . let us turn to the play of adolescents and adults, here education and work assume an ever increasing importance . . . there has to be an outlet for that fraction of aggression which has not been completely turned into useful work. That outlet is found in play . . . much of the energy that now goes into the more primitive, delinquent, and criminal behavior can be diverted into modified but none the less aggressive behavior in sports and games."

Many parents and teachers as well look upon mental illness as some bizarre morbid manifestation of funny or incongruous behavior. Mental illness may be very mild and innocuous and subtle; the many degrees, as well as forms are well explained by C. Macfie Campbell.[13] A disorder is mental, according to Doctor Campbell, if "its roots are mental. A headache indicates a mental disorder if it comes because one is dodging something disagreeable. A pain in the back is a mental disorder if its persistence is due to discouragement and a feeling of uncertainty and desire to have a sick benefit rather than to put one's back into one's work. Sleeplessness is a mental disorder if its basis lies in personal worries and emotional tangles. Many mental reactions are indications of poor mental health, although they are not usually classified as mental disorders. Discontent with one's environment may be a mental disorder, if its causes lie, not in some external situation, but in personal failure to deal with one's emotional problems. Suspicion, distrust, misinterpretation, are mental disorders when they are the disguised expression of repressed longings, into which the patient has no clear insight. Stealing sometimes indicates a mental disorder, the odd expression of underlying conflicts in the patient's nature; the feeling of fatigue sometimes, not overwork, but discouragement, inability to meet situations, lack of interest in the opportunities available. Unsociability, marital incompatibility, alcoholism, an aggressive and embittered social attitude may all indicate a disorder of the mental balance, which may be open to modification."

The teacher should be careful to teach the child that every-

[13] Campbell, C. Macfie, "Mental Hygiene in Industry," *Mental Hygiene*, July, 1921.

thing different is not abnormal, that much so-called abnormality is mediocrity, lack of initiative and dulling conservatism. The child should also be taught that extremism may be indicative of a healthy rather than an abnormal mind. Play should be conceived of as an expressive adventure. The exploring, seeking, reaching proclivities of the child should be given most sympathetic guidance and encouragement. A lack of interest or more specifically a misdirection and distortion of interest may be inimical to mental health. The ability to get along with others is a condition of good mental adjustment. Play may have a distinctive contribution to the alleviation of the evasions, timidity, fears, paucity of interest, social discomforts, lack of ease in group organization. The child who is timid in social relations may naturally awaken aggressive qualities in suitable selected play; the child whose interests are overbalancingly egotistic, may partially sublimate self and self ways in group play; the child who lacks ease in form of group organization most frequently finds comfort if taught to play understandingly with the group.

Some educators have called attention to what they consider to be adverse mental effects of conventional education upon the early development of the child. "One may observe," claims Doctor Matthais,[14] "the diminished trend of curves of growth in height or weight during the first school years." He continues to affirm that "this retardation of growth, manner in weight, in these first school years may be traced to neurosis due to the effect of restraint and exacting routine upon the psychically burdened child."

The first responsibility of education is to promote the normal growth and happy development of the child, and

[14] Matthais, E., "The Deeper Meaning of Physical Education," A. S. Barnes & Co., 1929, pp. 39-40.

teachers are becoming insistent that these functions remain unhampered.

It is most natural for us to canonize intelligence and to feel that intellectuality should be the distinguishing mark and accomplishment of our children. The sensible aim, however, from the standpoint of future health and happiness as well as efficiency in citizenship, is socialization. Socialization should be considered as the willing and understanding working of the part, with the whole. Man is by nature social. Even in the lower stages of animal life, social organizations have been developed. It is considered a sign of serious personality deviation for any individual to depart from the group coherence. The adaptation of the child from autistic thinking to progressive points of cooperation with others, the acceptance of ideas, plans and ideals of others enables the child to preserve a wholesome internal solidarity and thus to gain step by step in social spirit. He thus wants to become social because he feels that he is enabled in this way to express himself as well as aid in the expression of others.

If physical education is to assist in this social orientation of the child, it must, in the illuminating words of Jacks, represent "a finer technique than ordinary athletics, or gymnastics." It must be closely aligned with the natural early strivings and the later wholesome sublimations which is demanded of him.

It is well to realize right here that what his child seeks in play are outlets to satisfy wishes and yearnings which the environment, particularly the home circle stimulates. A patient friend of mine who is suffering from a severe form of mental illness becomes most antagonistic and resentful when the subject of play is mentioned. He is an artistic type and seeks cultural satisfaction in reading. In his early childhood, his parents had emphasized his intellectual capacity and stimulated his intellectual growth at the expense of development in play skills, and play appreciations. At the adolescent period when he desired greatly to play, he became conscious of his awkwardness and lack of skill as compared with his playmates. He then turned violently against play since it had at this stage of his experience proven to be a source of chagrin. The mistake which was made in the education of this patient is subtle and often made by parents and teachers unconsciously. Every child should be taught to express his words and feelings in action. In early youth many children express their imagination in many outlandish forms of play, frequently they are laughed at and as a result many repress these natural inclinations and lay the basis for harmful habits of excessive introspection. "Thought," says Durant, "is an instrument not an end; when it does not fulfill itself in action, it turns instead into a disease."

Every teacher of physical education should have opportunity to observe abnormal types in play, for from such study many most valuable and interesting clues may be obtained as to its effect upon personality. The organizing tendency of play is manifest in observing patient "Y" who is subject to epileptic seizures. Oftentimes between seizures he becomes overly active and excited, and is the victim of grandiose delusions. His activity becomes purposeless, scattered, and disorganized. He walks around in aimless fashion. When he is invited to play baseball, however, a definite change frequently takes place; he goes to the pitcher's base, concentrates his attention upon the batter, pitches the ball with fair control, utilizes simple elements of strategy and is able to organize his mental and physical powers so as to

[15] Durant, W., "Mansions of Philosophy," Simon and Schuster, 1929, p. 659.

produce a more unified although imperfect effort. One should not infer from this, however, that these organic cases are invariably stabilized by favorable psychogenic influences.

The physical director will also be impressed in noting the strength of the instinct of self-preservation in overcoming the many hysteriform positions and actions of the mentally sick individual. Patient "X" has the delusion that he must hold his arm in a rigid position in order to promote the necessary circulation; he holds the arm rigidly in fixed position for years until atrophy sets in. Once he is forcibly placed in the swimming pool, however, he strikes out and uses the arm in movement of almost normal extent. Patient "Z" drags one foot after another, appearing to the layman to have paralysis and being unable to lift his foot. Being placed in the deep water of the pool, he immediately begins to swim, and moves his leg almost normally. In these functional cases, automatic excitants stimulated them to overcome many counter impulses based upon unconscious motivation.

Then there is patient "A" who has lost practically all contact with normal experience. He lives in the fabrications of a subtly woven web of fantasy. Self-absorbed, he has no desire to again accept the responsibility of normal living. He sits day in and day out in useless passivity. He will not work and is gradually losing the ability to feed and dress himself. He is taken to a baseball field, a glove is placed on his hand, the ball is thrown to him; without comment he catches it and throws it back, continuing in this activity for hours at a time. After months and probably years, he may advance from this low level of activity to become an adept baseball player and the recognition he receives from this evidence of skill capacity may enhance his self-respect and enable him to branch out into more responsible things. The physical educator will be interested to know why it is that play has a distinctive capacity to awaken the interest of such a far regressed and introverted individual. The answer is difficult and conjectural. It is a well known fact that the mental impressions of early childhood remain and are more easily recalled than are the experiences of later life. There may be a deeper reason than this; pleasurable inciting emotions become associated with the early play activity and whereas, many of the emotions which normally attach themselves to our experience, become as a result of mental illness distorted, detached from their immediate relation and are lost, the emotions attaching themselves to these early experiences may remain to vitalize this play experience and stimulate its repetition.

Many interesting manifestations of a typical reaction to physical exercise are shown in the extremely nervous boy or girl. In children well balanced, the play mechanism operates smoothly and spontaneously. In these extremely nervous types, however, the automatic functions are interfered with and the play becomes halting and disconnected. This results from paying conscious attention to these automatic levels of action. The child who is unable to carry out ordinary play responses smoothly and who is continually straining and hesitating and inhibiting action, may possibly require treatment for some neurasthenic condition.

Morbid fears often upon the unconscious level complicate the problem.

A psychotic patient who had been a very skillful baseball player, would not play volley ball indoors and would give no reason for his refusing to do so. Finally one day when he made an attempt to play volley ball in the gymnasium, he became highly emotional and seemed almost paralyzed with fear; further examination disclosed the fact that he was afraid of closed spaces.

Another intelligent psychotic patient refused to take part in any form of exercise. Upon examination by the psychiatrist, he was found to have a delusion to the effect that his body was composed entirely of glass and would break if subjected to any excessive movement. Others of the paranoid type refuse to play because of imaginary enemies whom they feel will interfere with them or will injure them while playing. A large proportion who do not play, refuse to take part because of the social strain involved. These seclusive self-absorbed types feel that they will have to give up some of their coveted egocentric personality if they take part in group play. Many others are so wrapped up in their self-created world of fantasy that they have neither time nor inclination to enter the world of reality as typified in creative play. Others have grandiose ideas of importance and are unable to bend to the levels of comradeship and equality which play requires. Some, because of mood swings are either too excited or too depressed to play. Many because of confusion are unable to understand the necessary elements of play organization; and there are those who because of deep-seated feeling of inferiority believe that they are incapable and probably unwanted. A small proportion because of organic sickness and loss of necessary coordination are unwilling to take part. It must not be inferred from this, however, that the average psychotic patient does not take part in play; in fact, the reverse is true. There is no form of activity which will enlist as large a group of the mentally ill as does a highly diversified program of physical therapy, selected with careful reference to their physical, social, and personality levels.

All forms of mental illness are not as pronounced as

these just described. There are many forms of masking as physical disease. Oftentimes in play, the teacher notes evidences of crippling physical symptoms in pupils who, upon examination are entirely free from physical disease. It is not an uncommon thing, especially among nervous children, to note those who lose effective function of some part of the body as a result of a failure to meet the exacting demands of a too severe competitive relationship or of some other disagreeable situation which the child has been unable to overcome. This is shown in a great many cases when the boy or girl has a strong impulse to dominate others and seeks to control the behavior of other children who set up a strong defense reaction against him. Being unable to attain his desires he compensates for failure by some hysteriform reaction; he may simulate a sprained ankle which would justify him in leaving the game, or he may feign tiredness or complain about the athletic equipment. By many subtle evasions in overt conduct or through resort to rationalization, the frustrated child may seek satisfaction and the impressions he stores in these experiences may provide a source of future conflicts.

The inexperienced teacher may easily mistake mental copies of physical disease for the disease itself. The physical director not only has excellent opportunity to observe the mental distress resulting from such neurotic conduct, but is enabled to assist in the correction of these conditions by leading the child from undue introspection to a more objective understanding and action. The most effective utilization of play in mental hygienic practice, however, is in the direction of positive good health rather than in actual treatment. An ounce of prevention applies equally in these cases. The emphasis should be upon preventative building, rather than secondary readjustments.

One cannot understand the hygienic implications in play, if it is considered simply as a diversion. Play must serve greater purposes than this. It is generally conceded that calling the attention of the child to his nervous habits, simply accentuates them, making him conscious of his defects, may intensify them. Nervous reactions such as tics may be mitigated by interesting the child in zestful play. It should be understood, however, that these nervous symptoms are within the proper province of the psychiatrist. Devoting his conscious attention to the play activities and as his skill increases, concentrating his attention upon methods of strategy, may by these methods of sublimation reduce some neurotic symptoms. The final and adequate solution, however, must be made by the psychiatrist who will assist the child to recognize the basis of the disorder. Bertrand Russell,[16] "In the Praise of Idleness," reminds us, "our utilitarianism and specializing results have left most people in a lack of balance accompanied by some form of nervous disorder owing to failure to recognize that men as well as children have need of play, of periods of activity having no purpose beyond present enjoyment."

Delinquent behavior is fast being understood as a type of mental maladjustment. Some believe that the naturally aggressive outlets of the boy having been repressed, become distorted into anti-social channels. Clara Bassett[17] reminds us that "through sociological and statistical analysis of clinical findings on groups of cases, certain community problems, needs and defects, will stand out clearly as serious factors in the development of delinquent behavior among consider-

[16] Russell, Bertrand, "The Conquest of Happiness," Horace Liveright, Inc., 1933.
[17] Bassett, Clara, "Mental Hygiene in the Community," The Macmillan Company, 1934, p. 120. (By Permission of the Publishers.)

able numbers of children. Such defects may include a total lack of supervised play space and play facilities in one congested neighborhood."

The child should be placed in a situation in which he is able to realize the situation which comes from success as a result of reasonable effort. Clara Bassett [18] further reminds us that "the old system which makes no provision for various grades of mental ability, the dull or defective child is disastrously exposed to repeated failures which may permanently undermine his self-respect and self-confidence, habituate him to habits of evasion, deceit, inattention, or bluffing; cultivate an outlook of anxiety; hopelessness and despair result in the development of unhealthy compensatory behavior such as truancy, bullying, lying, or stealing."

While play experiences are replete with many opportunities for educational direction into wholesomely aggressive behavior, there is also the urge to make excuses probably due to an emphasis upon the competitive aspect. Many such rationalizations are so constantly employed in play that one may easily accept them as valid or laugh about them as humorous by-products. The girl playing tennis misses the ball out of bounds and then examines her racket with a critical eye, trying to fix the blame upon the racket. A baseball player misses a fly ball and immediately thereafter stops to examine his glove to discover the cause there. The ballplayer tries to pick up a "grounder" and after missing it, smooths out the ground and finds a small pebble and throwing it away directs the blame upon this outside condition. It seems a most natural tendency to lay the blame for failure to approach high standards upon the athletic equipment, clothing,

[18] Bassett, C., "Mental Hygiene in the Community," The Macmillan Company, 1934, p. 206. (By permission of the publishers.)

athletic field, court, or some other remote condition. The parent or teacher should not lose these opportunities to assist the child to take a more realistic and objective attitude, to accept the sense of failure as well as the exhilaration of success as part of the unified experience of playing.

We should seek to find the reason for the child's action; for example, if he lies about the score, is it due to fear of social disapproval for failure, a compensation for some felt want, or defect, or is it due to the mistake of parent or teacher in setting too high standards of accomplishment. The habit aspect of play should receive careful consideration; we must realize that the child adjusts to new situations upon the habit structure previously laid down. His conduct may be explained upon the habit organization of his feet and hands rather than the operation of the higher mental forces and ideals which we mistakenly feel are guiding his conduct.

If we could evoke and direct healthful emotions, the problem of the mental hygienic conduct of play would be solved. Play may most naturally produce mentally healthful states and wholesome situations because one event naturally follows another without hesitation, promise or threats; for example, in play suitably selected, the child experiences a succession of unhampered zestful acts, one after another. If he is warned about some conduct act, he thinks about it and may anticipate the punishment or the reward. Emotional states become awakened and develop into highly charged emotional feelings which may grow all out of proportion to the objective conditions of the situation. In play the action precedes more rationally and excessive emotions may not have time to overdevelop themselves.

This does not mean that play is without emotion. As everyone knows, play is fraught with many emotional yearnings and expressions. The pupil should be guided so that the play experience will develop the best and highest available emotional concomitants. The associations which play develops and which in turn develop play, become the excitants, provocatives, and buoyant accompaniments, of the play adventure. These stimuli vitalize play in adult life. Not only the play methods, styles and patterns which make up the mechanical form are repeated later on, but the emotional concomitants which make up the spirit of the play adventure attend the exercise and make it interesting, tiresome, irritating or obnoxious.

The personality of the child is most definitely illustrated in its play reactions. A number of different types may be observed; perverse, queer, frustrated, moody, lonely, stupid or crippled personalities may be reflected through the varied play situations. The child's integrated response to life, whether upon the "useful or useless side" to use Adler's phrase, may be detected in his play.

It is very probable that parents and teachers, in spite of their close observation and studious application to child guidance, do not for the most part, adequately envisage the child as a unity struggling for expression in an adult made and manipulated world. Repeatedly have the psychiatrists called attention to the necessity of getting upon the level of the child in order to see him in true educational perspective. Recreation should be conditioned as a most distinctive medium to assist the child so that he may avoid "unprofitable discontent and a sense of disproportion and incongruity with the environment." These feelings of disproportion and incongruity containing many elements of significant threat to a constructive integration of mental and bodily processes, may find their birth in a carelessly or poorly administered game as well as in other environmental relations. The play activity must be attuned to the many varieties and grades of individual fitness.

It is illuminating to realize that the child is tempted into modes of behaviour. He selects the type of conduct which brings him the most pleasure in the particular situation. And so the glamorous and yet constructive aspects of play should be kept before him. The destructive acts of the child which are the expressions of his protest against something or somebody can only be understood by examining the underlying cause. Hygienically administered play may bring constructive peacefulness after which comes orderliness and a reduction in the acts of destructiveness as the problem is resolved. The far and deep ramifications of play activities educationally conceived and presented may find a most important place in this field of psychic adjustment.

BIBLIOGRAPHY

The Inner World of Childhood, Frances C. Wickes, New York, D. Appleton-Century Co., 1927. A study by the aid of the Jungian Psychology of the constitution of the child's unconscious level and its function.

Introduction to Psychoanalysis for Teachers, Anna Freud, London. George Allen and Unwin, Ltd. (Translated by B. Low), 1931. A fundamental for an understanding of the significance and the functioning of the unconscious through behaviour.

Difficulties in Child Development, Mary Chadwick, New York. John Day, 1928. A psychoanalytic interpretation of special and every day problems of child development.

Psychoanalysis and Medicine, The Wish To Fall Ill, Karin Stephen, Cambridge University Press, London, 1935. A study of the operation of the unconscious and its relationship to conduct and conduct disorders with an excellent discussion of the constitution of the unconscious and its laws of operation.

The Psychology of Insanity, Bernard Hart, Cambridge, The University Press, 1925. The classic psychological interpretation of the main mechanisms of mental illness. An important fundamental for the hygienically conscious teacher.

The Major Symptoms of Hysteria, Pierre Janet, New York, Macmillan Company, 1920. The teacher learns from this scholarly and authoritative presentation many of the symptom signs of the child which may lay the basis for the hysterical coloring of many play maladjustments.

Outlines of Psychiatry, William A. White, Washington, D. C., Mental and Nervous Disease Publishing Co., 1926. An elementary textbook acquainting the teacher with the major mental disease entities, their manifestations, symptoms and treatment. A most valuable psychological orientation for the teacher.

Mental Hygiene and Education, Mandel Sherman, New York, Longmans, Green and Co., 1934. An illuminating discussion of the psychiatric problems in education with many informative references to the role of play in hygienic health.

Principles and Practise of Recreational Therapy for the Mentally Ill, John Eisele Davis in collaboration with William R. Dunton, Jr., New York, A. S. Barnes and Company, 1936. A scientific exposition of the utilization of recreation as a therapeutic adjuvant in the modern treatment of mental illness.

Mental Health, Frank E. Howard and Frederick L. Patry, New York, Harper and Brothers, 1937. A clear cut and comprehensive exposition of the principles and practise of mental health with emphasis on the treatment of mental deviations. The chapter on Objective Psychology (Adolf Meyer's approach) is illuminating to the teacher.

The Wholesome Personality, William H. Burnham, New York, D. Appleton-Century Co., 1932. An interpretation of behaviour as the result of an integration of mental and bodily processes. A most able hygienic approach to the problems of education and recreation.

The Human Mind, K. A. Menninger, New York, Knopf, 1930. A most interestingly written exposition of the psychology of mental functioning, with many plain illustrations and special references to mental abnormality.

The Nervous Child, Hector C. Cameron, Oxford University Press, 1929. A thorough and sympathetic treatment of the mental and psychological problems and adjustments in childhood.

Individual Differences, Frank E. Freeman, New York, Holt, 1934. The development of individual differences in intellectual and mental capacities and interests. Important orientation in determining standards and objectives in physical education, in which many mental conflicts result from standards of achievement based upon mistaken postulates.

The Road to Adolescence, Joseph Garland, M.D., Cambridge, Harvard University Press, 1934. Chapters of special interest to physical educators and hygienists on: nutrition and diet, fatigue, care of the body and the handicapped child.

ARTICLES

Fear of Action as an Essential Element in the Sentiment of Melancholia. P. Janet, Feelings and Emotions, The Wittenberg Symposium, Clark University Press, 1928. A most informative discussion of the action field of the individual in relationship to states of hysteria, presaging the importance of associating activity in the early life of the child with wholesome interpretations and constructive emotional concomitants. Of fundamental significance to the teacher of physical education.

The Compensatory Function of Make Believe Play, E. S. Robinson, Psychological Review, 1920, 27, pp. 205-214. The role of phantasy in preparing the child for more responsible levels of thinking and acting.

Chapter II

PLAY AND

ADJUSTMENT TO THE

OUTSIDE WORLD

PLAY AND THE CHILD'S LANGUAGE

THE SIGNIFICANCE of physical education to child guidance is partially explained by Piaget as reported by Burnham in "The Wholesome Personality." Piaget discovers, between the ages of six and seven, two levels of thought, one above the other. The lower plane is made up of associations growing out of the child's own wants. "It is the plane of subjectivity, of desires and whims, of the Lust Prinzip," as Freud would say. In contradistinction to the lower subjective plane is the objective level, in which the less tangible functions of the child's life, such as thinking and talking, take place. The significance of play in child guidance at this period is evident from Piaget's words, which lead to the conclusion that children before the age of seven or at seven do not understand thoughts communicated through vocal utterance. Ideas must be expressed in action if the child is to achieve an adequate realization of their meaning.

The teacher is naturally concerned with the aim of investigating the child's play life with its most natural, spontaneous and pleasurable experience and condition it for the child so that he can attach the most wholesome signs and symbols. This leads to the association of constructive attitudes with the play experience. For example, it is very necessary that the nursery teacher should take the toys which he is giving to the child for the first time and use them in the child's presence in the proper and constructive ways and while using them in this manner to give expression to the pleasurable, emotional responses which the situation should normally provoke. While playing in this manner, teachers and others should be careful to use the proper words describing the play equipment and the states produced. In this way wholesome associations may be formed. The child will thus be able to understand and employ these simple constructive symbols while growing into reality. The relationship, however, of one symbol to another and meaning of the more complex symbols may not be fully understood by those who use them and may easily lead to conflicts. The important point for the teacher in this connection is that the play tools and play experiences have much to do with the early language formation of the child. A happy play life properly directed will result in a bright play language and associated words and symbols of constructive relation to mental health.

All the while, the child, wandering and growing into reality, is accepting signs and symbols and making language images of his environment. The development of the child's language is one of the ways through which he approaches and understands the world about him. The unique contribution of play in this situation is appreciated when we realize that the child's symbolism is largely gleaned and organized from his play experiences. These associations affect most profoundly his present and future understanding and evaluation of experience and of conduct. Simple play symbols may take on complex and not casually related associations leading frequently to conflicts. And, in exceptional cases, these symbolic representations may become so elaborated and complex that only a careful psychoanalytic examination is able to unravel them.

There is probably no better opportunity to create healthy symbolic associations than through suitably presented play. The essential fairness and openness of these play experiences tend to create associations of the nobler and more wholesome sentiments which may be irradiated into individual play experiences and play toys and other paraphernalia. For example, the baseball bat, while potentially an implement for sustaining injury to player, becomes potentially and definitely associated with "hit the ball rather than the person." In conducting baseball games with most far regressed psychotic patients, I have never seen these mentally sick individuals who have even lost much of their formal training, and understanding, use the bat as a weapon or threaten a fellow player with it. Early play experience has established wholesome attitudes which remain while many other normal traits and associations are lost.

It is most interesting to note the growth of the child's language through his play experience. At the close of infancy as he begins to vocalize, he realizes a more definite communication than the cries and signs by which he formerly attempted to gain and convey meaning. Branching out into childhood, he gains ideas from his playmates and in attempting to understand their language and build up the most effective means of communication, enlarges his associative sphere.

The six hundred words which the average child learns between the ages of two and three are most intimately connected with new experiences in helping himself. His growing powers bring new and glowing experiences and his language becomes most significantly connected with his play experiences. Many words find their inciting association in pleasurable or painful play activities. His total vocabulary at 3 years includes eight or nine hundred words including pronouns, plurals and the past tense. He attempts to describe his play both real and make-believe. He can, at this age period, play games involving two processes, he can put two parts of a severed picture together. Learning some color names, he is much attracted by play involving colors and attempts matching of similar colors.

At the age of eight, the average child is in the third grade. He begins to expand his language and uses "every part of speech and form of sentence" and on the whole his speech has taken on a mature character. He is quick to see inconsistencies in the conduct of play. He becomes critical of inexact methods and inaccurate statements. While his motor control and skill in the manipulation of toys is increasing, his plans and ideas are far in advance of this ability and his language tends to become broadened into generalities and heightened into idealism.

At the age of thirteen, "The Birthday of the Imagination," the play language becomes even more idealistic and at the same time more discernibly realistic. Mental and physical spurts produce intra-psychic conflicts, and these difficulties are increased by wide variations which develop between different individuals and within the individuals themselves. Play terminology utilizes slang and bright unconventional sayings. A pseudo-aggressiveness characterizes much group play with complicating extremes of indecision and hesitancy. Some children are extremely mature and well coordinated at this period, while others are physically and intellectually immature. This wide range of deviation should be carefully considered in guiding play activities and attempting to understand the wide diversity of language employed by the adolescent in play.

Froebel's words, "the plays of children are the germinal leaves of all later life," refer most probably to the influence of the play language as well as the play acts. The associations which make up idiographic development of the child through play experiences, however, may contain harmful as well as beneficial elements. For example, the words which the child associates with the baseball bat may be charged with an unpleasant emotional symbolism because he was not able to hit the ball with his bat in the presence of other children who were more successful than he was, or because he has perceived unwholesome experiences of the others attempting to play the game. In after years when the adult has outgrown the period of actual playing, he has thrust upon him through the newspapers, conversation and radio many and valid references to baseball. The uncomfortable or antagonistic feeling which he experiences, may come from these early associations. Emotions as well as acts are learned and the modern parent as well as teacher should seek to invest the early play experience of the child with most wholesome values and constructively rich associations.

"BE YOUR AGE"

"The child," says Will Durant, "is among many wonderful potentialities capable of that ultimate mystery, growth." The child's growth is indeed an entrancing mystery and the teacher who can envisage these developmental cycles through which he develops into different people from yesterday, today, tomorrow, and the day after will understand some of the secrets of his evolutionary behavior contributing to his present conduct.

Adler's belief that the behavior style of child life is fixed after it is four or five years old and cannot be easily changed is gaining evidence in educational circles today. What Adler meant to convey was the habit of behavior or prototype is laid down in these early years and the subsequent conduct represents a continuous effort in the adjustment of this basic pattern to reality.

Educators have discovered a significant relationship between animal intelligence and length of the period of infancy. Man has the longest period of infancy, the longest opportunity for learning responses, receiving impressions and laying down the behavior pattern which exerts such a strong and compelling influence upon adult behavior.

Will Durant gives the interesting changes from youth to middle age and on to old age. The instinct of youth expressed as raw activity in a game becomes refined into rational induction in middle age, and deduction in old age. Frequently the middle aged parent mistakenly emphasizes the necessity of youth to play in a more studied manner and the grandparents mistakenly attempt to convince youth of the importance of reducing play to logical formulas. The innovation of youth may become the habit of middle age and the custom of old age. While youth clamors for new ways of doing things, the middle aged parent may emphasize the habit aspects of the game and the elderly members of the household may insist upon the conventionalities. The child will emphasize the play nature of the adventure while the middle aged individual may think of it in terms of work and the elderly individual in terms of rest. The child may develop art in play, the middle aged individual science, and the elderly person religion. The child through play may develop his imagination, the parent his intellect, and the grandparent his memory. The child may be interested in theory, the parent knowledge and the elderly person in wisdom. The philosophical outlook of the child in play may be represented by optimism, while the view of the middle aged may be that of meliorism while pessimism may dominate old age. Youth may be radical in play; middle age, liberal, and old age, conservative. The child is anxious to know what will happen in the future, middle age seeks discipline and old age authority. The child seeks vacillation, mature age seeks stability and old age may find stagnation. The application of all this is best expressed in the aphorism "be your age." While the child should be viewed as a growing animal, it should not be expected to act as an adult. One of the most difficult problems to surmount in teaching play to children is to avoid setting standards in terms of the abilities and interests of the teacher rather than the abilities and interests of the child. It is a common mistake for the adult to construe the imaginative excursions of the child in terms of intellectual process while the elderly individuals may view them purely from vantage point of memory.

Twins, Johnny and Jimmy, illustrate how attitudes toward play in early life may produce wholesome or unwholesome behavior traits. Johnny was stimulated to undertake motor activities which he was capable of doing at regular intervals. Jimmy was deliberately restricted and allowed to remain in crib. A study of their behavior began 22 days after birth until 26 months. A month after the end of experiment, Johnny still retained the skills developed in running, jumping and skating while Jimmie's attitude showed retrogression; he was fearful and timid. Johnny's physical weight and development was greater than his brother's.

The teacher of physical education should study carefully

the genetic development of the child. The baby depends upon his parents as he is helpless. He soon finds that he can do some things unassisted and gains much pleasure in the realization of these new accomplishments. The parents' attitude changes; they are made happy by the newly acquired movements of the child and may emphasize these accomplishments rather than the things they themselves do for him. With physical growth of the child, motor capacity and interest unfold and parents develop many fears that he may injure himself in the exercise of his newly discovered capacity. Parental admonition and restrictions then take their place in the education of the child. If the child is to do things satisfactorily at this stage, he must unconsciously adopt a most wholesome attitude toward the process of growth and the increasingly pressing demands of reality. The difficulties encountered are to be viewed as pleasurable ventures into new worlds. Confused in an adult-made world, beset by different sources of authority of school, church relatives, parents, personal experience and personal interpretations, imbalances of mood and effect, the child reaches out to the source that is most conducive to his pleasure and his understanding.

The relationship of play activities to the chronological age is shown by Doctor Furfey. The six-year-old enjoys dramatic play and is interested mostly in toys utilized in physical activity, he likes to play active games.

The eight-year-old has become self-assertive and is interested in games involving individual competition, complicated group game and gang activities are not evident as yet.

The ten-year-old likes team games, fifty percent of the children of this age show a readiness to join groups; boys have a tendency to join play with girls.

The twelve-year-old has reached the typical gang age; his

interests are characterized by restless activity. He takes part readily in team games and develops an interest in checkers, cards and so on.

The fourteen-year-old grouping is not homogeneous in its interest. The fourteen-year old is rapidly approaching physical and mental maturity and his interests depend upon these and other conditions, some are like the twelve-year old and others like the sixteen-year old.

The sixteen-year-old has reached the stage of definite interests in the opposite sex, he likes athletics of the more mature form, his individuality causes conflicts between him and his parents and teachers. From these findings, Furfey concludes that there is a slowly developing process of maturity which cannot be measured in terms other than the child's interests and activity.

Many educators have attempted to present a classification showing the child's interests at various ages. Lee believes that the creative impulse begins to assert itself during the first three years. From three to six is the age of impersonation; six to eleven the big Indian or age of self-assertion; eleven to fourteen, age of loyalty, and fourteen to twenty-one, the apprentice age. Henry Curtis believes that the age up to six represents the imaginative stage, from six to puberty represents the big Indian stage and from puberty on, the stage for team games. Croswell believes that from six to nine, the child uses symbolic objects, from nine to thirteen is characterized by vigorous exercise of the whole body and from fourteen and on, the creative spirit prevails.

In the sensory development of the child there is first a period of grasping in which the rattle, pyramids, wooden beads or rag doll supply the object, then there comes the feeling of colored cubes, ball, teddy bear, sandpile and shovel. Then there is a period of listening to the drum, pot and spoon, radio and there is the zestful sensation of lifting large hollow blocks; then the motor development is helped by pushing nursery chairs, kiddy car, or barrel and pulling wagon, cardboard box and toys. Then comes climbing on the indoor climbing apparatus, ladder, jungle jim tree. The next step is balancing; walking, using balancing board, wheelbarrow and this is followed by running with the assistance of kiddy car and other paraphernalia.

The development of motor control by the child is a subject whose entrancing interest is equalled by its hygienic import.

At twelve weeks the average child begins to take notice of objects, at twenty weeks he grasps blocks, at twenty-four weeks he grasps two blocks and puts one on top of the other. These progressive patterns of play behavior continue with growth until at three years he can bring the blocks into combinations. From three years the child seems to be outgrowing babyhood and shows rapidly developing capacities and interests in play. He has gained increased speed and skill. He walks faster and talks more clearly. He can climb stairs without support and gradually commences walking by using alternate steps. He gains much pleasure by hopping on one foot. He can copy straight and horizontal lines. He may begin to use his right hand more than his left in manipulating objects. He begins to enjoy dramatic play, to play more with others and less by himself, he tries new things and employs more complex methods. This is the period when he gets into everything and his widening explorations lead to many painful contacts which produce associations and inhibitions of significance in hygienic development. Play methods, toys and the play environment should be conditioned insofar as is practical, of course, so that the child can gain a sense of security and pleasure in his newly developed zest for activity.

Unfavorable emotional disturbance can easily result from misunderstanding or indifference at this stage. Toys should be suited to his stage of growth as well as his interests since many inhibitions and fears are created by ill considered play material and inadequately conceived methods which interfere with the most wholesome integration of the child in later years.

The eight-year-old period is less emotional than the preceding or succeeding one. Interest for competition increases; cooperative and social games are played but there is a strong self-sufficiency which makes many parents and teachers feel that he is unresponsive to play. Proper motivating emotional stimuli does not attach itself to childhood acts which the adult deems of importance. For example, the child is not interested in personal cleanliness. Teachers will be wise to lay but little emphasis at this period, upon cleanliness in play but will wait until the promptings of adolescence make him inwardly ready for an appreciation and practice of this health habit. His social development is largely through play. He becomes uncompromising in his likes and dislikes. He forms many of his values, ideas and ideals from the standards laid down in the conduct of his playmates and these values are most frequently considered of more value to him than the social graces emphasized by parent or teacher. The former he often invests with ideas of utility and the latter with the odium of niceties. He finds zestful spirit in self-imposed conformity to group organization. The social spirit is developing and the social values in games provide usable educational material. The child is beginning at this stage to look upon these group relationship values as important and the teacher should employ them to assist the player in wholesome adjustment to other people. He is varying his social life and is developing through the selection of new experiences and things. Play organized with an understanding of these conditions can be of distinctive benefit.

The thirteen-year period brings increasingly difficult adjustments. There are often intra-psychic conflicts and antagonisms between home and outside influences. Boys become interested in girls as members of the opposite sex, girls become "appearance conscious." Group differentiations and group interests develop more strongly and play is heavily tinctured with ideas and ideals of loyalty. The adolescent often prides himself upon putting group interest before personal interest. Play at this period should utilize the genetic development of these unfolding altruistic qualities. The willingness to adjust to the needs and necessities of others, to sublimate egotistic cravings into the higher demands of the group—the adolescent is "inwardly ready" for such social transfer values in play. He will get much substantial enjoyment out of the recreational experiences which include unselfish service to others and personal responsibility for larger social tasks and wider appreciations of the desires and strivings of others; in short, he has reached the opportune stage for the acceptance of these higher social values and the teacher should take advantage of this favorable cycle in educational practise.

The child grows not only in physical ways but adds from day to day actions and associations which lay the foundation for habit formations. As it has been pointed out repeatedly by educators, these habit structures usually make or break the child. The physical educator should note carefully those attitudes and types of conduct which activate the child into desirable play and those which appear to separate him from these activities and relegate him to the role of spectator or cynic. Such behaviour patterns should be studied in relation to the child's whole makeup. Very significant habits of participation or non-participation may be formed and will undoubtedly have much to do with the future adjustment of the child to adult responsibilities and to the growing problems of reality. The effect of wholesome participation upon growth and wholesome mental integration is self-evident. The child may develop into a predominantly outgrowing or ingrowing individual or introvert or extravert personality.

The hyperactive child should receive careful study by parent and teacher. Youth is active and the healthy child bubbles over with energy. Abundance of energy is a natural endowment of the young child. The teacher may, however, easily make a mistake of confusing the natural high spirit of the child with types of abnormal hyperactivity. Distorted speed of movement may show some pathological condition and may represent some conflict from which he is seeking to escape, some thwarted desire he wishes to attain or an endocrine imbalance may possibly be the cause of excessive and distorted activity. These hyperactive children should receive the attention of the psychiatrist.

Parents and teachers should build up a wholesome rapport with the child by growing along with him, "growing," says Samuel Crothers,[1] "is like falling, it is all right so long as you keep on; the trouble comes when you stop." Little Johnny digs a trench in the sand and creates a castle surrounded by a protecting moat. In phantasy he adds knights to protect himself from an invading horde. To the teacher he recounts the story of his great adventure. The understanding and contributing sympathy of older children helps him build up his childhood experience and the integrating acumen of the teacher balances all the elements of this happy experience into cooperative understanding; thus, the light of

[1] Crothers, Samuel M., "The Ignominy of Being Grown Up," Houghton Mifflin and Co., 1908.

age clears the way for the romping happiness of childhood and the music of children's patter enters into a symphony of educational understanding. Some play situations lose their distinguishing zest, however, because the inexperienced teacher views the child's play in terms of physical expression and even adult growth. It is for the psychiatrist and psychologist to more clearly and adequately emphasize the qualities which accentuate and vitalize recreation. These qualities are the interests and motives of the child. We should look upon them as young adventurers exploring the wide world. We should see this process as a harmonious endeavor. And the world's busy inattention in its sombre overtones should not destroy this happy note of the child's answer to experience through his play adventures.

THE IMPULSE TO BE ATTRACTIVE

Mary was the kind of a girl one finds in any large group, a fairly agreeable and bright student, somewhat of a dreamer but well acquainted and interested in current happenings. She lived in a sleepy, small and conventional town which gave her but little encouragement for branching out. She seemed, however, anxious to get away from something or someone, and struggled rather feebly and ineffectively, for something seemed to hold her down. In a quiet conversation with a number of friends, she talked in a reserved fashion; among others, however, she was not completely at ease, she lacked that girlish spontaneity, zest, and personal confidence. She was most unhappy about this lack of naturalness and described it to her inability to become attractive. The more she attempted to correct the situation, the more sensitive she became, and the greater her feeling of inadequacy. She felt that people noticed her attempts to improve her efforts.

Her problem concerned the family very much. A discerning mother sent her to a boarding school blessed by a teacher well grounded in practicable principles of mental hygiene. Mary's personality problem became clear to the teacher. She made no direct attempts to treat her feelings of inadequacy but outlined many direct methods of analysis and suggestions. It was observed that she could play tennis well and this aptitude was stressed. She was encouraged to participate in school tournaments and received much favorable comment in the school publication for her skillful playing. The discerning and sympathetic teacher called Mary's attention to her improvement in poise, color and posture. She began to play tennis with boys and was soon admired because of her physical dexterity and grace. One of her boy partners became unusually attentive toward her and took her to dances and the theatre. These experiences of satisfaction had a most significant effect upon Mary's personality. She felt that she was wanted, that she had a place in the social scheme, that she had become attractive; she then became more anxious to associate herself with other people. A more wholesomely integrated and more happy personality was built up.

In this case as the hygienist observed, a failure to increase the self-respect of Mary would have meant failure in the accomplishment of the most important additional goal, all other things were secondary to this. Direct methods simply serve to bring the sore to constant attention and aggravate the situation. A failure in readaptation would have meant that Mary would have undoubtedly reconstructed her personality upon a lower and even more exclusive basis, retiring into a self-imposed limitation of social passivity. Mental institutions are full of such types as Mary who are unable to find some means of correcting a morbid feeling of personality inadequacy. The personality poise which comes from physical grace and all-round attractiveness presents many of the vital elements for mental confidence and mental health; muscular control is indirectly related to social expression, healthful beauty to social posture, the glamor of alert eyes combined with vivacious color may well add to the foundation for the aggressive attitudes which bespeak a wholesome mental integration. A correct posture may have much to do in establishing mental as well as physical balance. Illustrations of many mental hygienic experiences are given by Kirkpatrick: [2] "Peggy was a senior in high school. Ever since she started school she has excelled in whatever she undertook to do. Her marks always placed her scholastically at the head of her class, and her ability on the tennis court was more than outstanding. She had never been beaten at the game and had an idea that she knew all there was to know about it. When Peggy arrived at camp, she was made leader of her bunk. But the first morning on the tennis court put an end to her high opinion of her tennis. All her life she had merely been playing—playing for the sake of winning. Now she was greeted by the counselor in charge by a new idea, that of playing for the sake of playing well, playing in perfect form. Peggy knew nothing about the correct form of playing, and found in her first hour on the courts that she had much to learn. Playing tennis in form, then, became her main purpose in life, and her specialty while in camp. Many were the battles she had with herself, and many were the mornings she arose early to get in some private practice before the rest of the camp was awake. At the close of the summer, Peggy was a different personality. Instead of the 'know-it-all' Peggy who had arrived in June, she was now the Peggy with the desire to know more about her favorite sport. All

[2] Kirkpatrick, E. A., "Mental Hygiene for Effective Living," D. Appleton-Century Company, 1934, pp. 302-3.

summer she specialized in tennis; all summer she found out more and more how little she really knew about the thing in which she thought she excelled; and all summer she was developing individuality which at the close of eight weeks marked her as the girl who played an excellent game of tennis, but who still felt she had much to learn.

"Helen was born with a harelip. All of her life she had been very self-conscious, timid at mixing with other girls, and reluctant at joining them in their games. She was fourteen when we first met her in camp. From the time she was five years old she had been to a private school where she had almost individual attention, and where other children were much less likely to talk about her infirmity or to make fun of her. It was after much anxious thought and consideration that her parents decided to send her to camp, and even when they left her, they expected Helen would shortly ask to be taken home feeling left out by the other girls. For the first day, it was difficult for her to make friends, and the other campers were rather hesitant about approaching her, so very noticeable was her deformity. Those who did talk with her did it solely out of the kindness of their hearts, and it was evident that they felt sorry for her and were trying to make her feel at home. Soon, however, she learned to swim, to ride horseback, to play tennis, and to canoe, and at the close of camp she was voted one of the best all-around girls at camp. No camper received more hearty applause when they received the camp letter as the highest award possible, than did Helen. No girl had a sweeter disposition and no one was more willing to help out. She was a changed girl when her parents came to take her home at the close of eight weeks. Nor does the story end here. During the winter when the applications came in for camp the following summer, several girls asked to be put in the bungalow with Helen. Her deformity which was very marked made no difference.

"Mary had a glass eye which had to be removed every night before retiring. This process of course made her very self-conscious and might perhaps have made her an outcast with the other girls if it hadn't been for the careful camp supervision which finally discovered that Mary could play a trumpet exceptionally well. Here was a chance to develop this girl's individuality, and the result was that all the unpleasantness of the glass eye was forgotten by the other campers, and Mary became known as the girl who could play the trumpet so well that every one wanted to hear her."

THE HEROIC ASPECTS OF PLAY IN HYGIENIC RELATIONSHIP

Do you remember when as a child you went to a baseball game and saw a fleetfooted outfielder speed over the ground, make a spectacular dive into the air and stab a fast driven ball? This incident awakened a vivid and happy imagination and when you came home you grabbed a ball and glove and played yourself as if pleasantly impelled by some strong yet mysterious force. Upon more mature reflection you realized that the subtle stimulation resulted from seeing someone perform an act associated with the heroic. The heroic acts and attitudes attained through play contain many elements and significant forces of mental hygienic import. The play experience if it is to be meaningful to your child must above all be inspirational as well as zestful.

A most illuminating illustration of play as composed of many elements of heroism which capture the imagination and interest of the child and which may be directed into wholesome hygienic influences is provided in the character of every boy's idol "Babe" Ruth. "Babe" Ruth played the game with sympathy, zest and love. The children admired and loved him because he met them in their own world. "He is just like us kids," a boy said after Ruth had signed the numerous autographs for children as was his daily custom. He adopted the frank, direct, incisive language so natural to the child. Speaking of his retirement due to old age, he said, "I am going to take things easy, if I get bored I can always get out to a vacant lot and play ball with a bunch of kids." The spirit of true play was so infectious in his playing, S. J. Woolf says in the New York *Times*, "His prowess caught the imagination of the nation; to ragamuffin as well as scholar, to rotund business man as well as debutante, 'Babe' Ruth became a hero. Candy and clothes were named for him; articles signed by him were printed throughout the country; hard wallops in other sports were described by his name and his round face with its broad nose and heavy lips became as well known as a blue bell on a telephone. No tale of ancient monarch has more romance attached to it than the 'Babe' Ruth Saga."

The ideal of millions of children, the character of "Babe" Ruth illustrated the intensity and radiation of the play spirit emanating from a picturesque and powerfully unique personality; its integrating force in capturing popular acclaim and welding public opinion of the child and adult world as well.

The richness and depth of the experience of this orphan from poverty to a salary exceeding that of the president of the United States—is replete with most significant clues and lures to a more hygienic appreciation of the integrating phenomena of the play spirit. The big brother, kindly and unassuming attitude, the sincere and childish love for simple things, the strong and aggressive temper when in a baseball game, weaknesses and foibles of "following the horses," his subsequent glorious reform when made to understand that the kids of the United States were looking to him as their hero and prototype, his powerful physique strengthened by a most generous attitude, the heroic temper, a translation into gallant and chivalrous favors for children—all these elements created a most loving and loved personality. Every child old enough to read was stirred by the mighty exploits of the "King of Swat" and every home run which rang from his bat found a jubilant response in the hearts of millions of boys who identified themselves with him in many significant associations. That play is not an intellectual exploit, a strategic creation of cold calculation or hard muscles, but a thing of the heart and spirit is another lesson we learn from this remarkable career.

BOYS AND GIRLS AT PLAY

Among the most essential adjustments boys and girls must make in both school and society is a healthful heterosexual relationship. In the pre-school period they are not so conscious of sex barriers and a most wholesome integration of the sexual growth with the social conventionalities may be produced by the understanding teacher of physical training through properly administered play for mixed groups. Types of play should be selected, methods employed and a philosophy taught which will enable the participant to appreciate the activity as a cooperative group enterprise in which impulses of the sexes may find wholesome socialization. The showing off of the boy, a process often emerging from a sense of physical superiority should be directed into channels of higher sublimation. The submissive qualities of the girls, likewise have their sexual significance and should be observed with a view to their most wholesome guidance. Superiority of boys over girls should not be made the aim of such mixed play nor the dominance of either sex the goal. The contribution which each may make to the higher socialized concept of recreation provides a most worthy objective.

"I am coming to believe," says John Rathbone Oliver, "that this early segregation of the sexes is an artificial thing, that boys and girls should not and need not be divided into two separate groups at such an early age. We are constantly impressing on our boys the fact that they are boys and not girls. The boy's mind is inoculated at an early age with the concept that he belongs to the superior sex. They must lift the taboos that separate girls from boys at an age when neither is naturally conscious of any such distinction, that assign to each sex barriers of activity and of self-expression which may not be crossed except at the cost of constant rebuke and criticism."

A striking illustration of the damaging effect of early segregation of boys and girls in school comes to my mind. A patient suffering from mental illness with whom I come in daily contact, complains most bitterly because he was not allowed to play with the girls in his early education, and in attempting to explain the reasons for this, he ascribes all sorts of fictitious beliefs and fantastic causes. He claims he should have been brought up as "people" and not as a boy without play relationships with the girls of his own age. The socializing of the sex impulses is the most important goal of education and hygiene. It is agreed by many educators that boys and girls should be encouraged to play together, but many sex differences should be taken into account. Small girls are more likely to play with dolls, housekeeping, and so on, while small boys are more likely to play Indians, bandit, cowboy or robber games. Girls are more patient than boys in their play experiences and can stand monotonous types of play better. Girls generally are more interested in games involving visiting, reading, writing, et cetera. Boys naturally play more active games than girls. Girls do not participate in games requiring as much organization as do boys. Girls are more interested in play forms associated with the home life or in relatively restricted rules of action; picnics, gathering flowers, et cetera. The girls differ from boys in their play interests existing between the ages of $8\frac{1}{2}$ to $10\frac{1}{2}$ inclusive, and with the increase of chronologic age, boys and girls tend to engage more frequently in like activities. The more extensive range of the boys' activity as compared with the girls' is possibly due to the fact that play represents to the boy the gamut of the adult's competitive world in which he must prepare himself. The girls unemancipated until today do not have this motivation for enlarged activity during the period previous to entering school.

Boys and girls are quite similar in many respects in both ability and interests and can play with pleasure and benefit many of the same activities. There is a difference, however, not only in the capacity for play but a difference in the various ways in which boys and girls play. Boys find a greater urge for competitive games. Boys are more aggressive in their games than girls. While girls prefer more conservative types, girls are more emotional, generally more tender and sympathetic. Boys are more interested in the large things, girls more interested in small details. Durant[3] states the difference between the social instincts of the two sexes:

[3] Durant, W., "The Mansions of Philosophy," Simon and Schuster, 1929, p. 180.

"In the group of instincts which we have just surveyed—the instincts that preserve the individual—man's superiority is manifest and natural. But in the instincts that preserve the group, woman is as superior as in the instincts that preserve the race. She is more social and more sociable; she likes company and multitudes, and surrenders herself with delight to the anonymity of crowds. She is a gregarious animal."

PLAY AND WORK

One of the most important among the many adjustments which the child must take to the growing world of reality, is the transformation from the play level to work responsibility. From a mental hygienic standpoint this change should be gradual and be vitalized by happiness and sustained by understanding. The spontaneous desire with which a child plays should serve to motivate work. If this attitude could be transferred from the one activity to the other, a most important adjustment to a major problem of mental hygiene would be rendered less difficult. The child has always wanted to play. The play environment reflecting the racial and national ideals of time and place has represented an evolution from religious, economic and social institutions to the liberal ideals of the present century. The economic change has been no less significant, products are now produced with little physical effort and the requirements of personnel in the manufacture of goods has greatly decreased with the resultant added leisure of adults. Child labor is fast passing from the scene of great social advances and experimentations.

Recreation as a component of work in hygienic application may be critically explained in this manner: the life of every individual is made up of significant accents upon activity. There is a period of intense and hard application followed by a period of abandon of stresses and relaxations. The difference between the two is a difference of kind as well as degree. In the intense phase, one endeavors to prescribe action through rationalization and finding that the human mechanism cannot live by mind alone there follows a relaxing phase of play, oftentimes of indifferentiated types. The attitude of understanding all as a basis of action is supplanted by an attitude of physical abandon in which mere intellectual guidance is set aside and the physical organism combines with the emotional to express itself in expansive trends.

There is probably no more effective means of developing the personality than the doing of constructive tasks which in the mind of the doer are worthwhile. Many hygienic lessons can be gleaned in such natural progression from play to work. The child should be taught zestful work and play processes as naturally embodied in his progressive development. Nor should cultural values be divorced from play and work. It is a most important thing for the child to understand that the body is not inferior to the mind and that the development of the body may be a cultural and creative activity of the highest order. Neither should the mercenary aspect be advanced as the controlling criterion of work accomplishment. A little child reflecting the attitude of his parents explained, "Our baby is the best that money can buy." The child soon learns that those who work the hardest do not necessarily obtain the highest place in the community.

The difference in fatigue induced by work and play is most important. The recreational director should be acquainted with the theory of the motivation-fatigue relationship even though he cannot explain this difference. Patrick affirms that the more recently acquired mental capacities of the race such as concentration and analysis bring about rapid fatigue and that this can be overcome by returning to the elemental big muscle activities which are acquired earlier in racial experiences.

The happy road from play to responsibility is often made easy by chores. Work vitalized by zestful attitudes may become most valuable recreation losing thereby the ennui which makes it at times monotonous and damaging to a well poised and relaxed personality. The colloquial word, chores, describes a form of work and play activity pregnant with mental health promise. Little odd pieces of everyday business tactfully turned into cooperative enterprise, the fulfillment of which requires no unreasonable amount of time or labor and the doing of which makes the child feel a kinship of loving responsibility toward the common weal. The child feels that he is worthwhile and necessary to a larger circle than a selfish egocentric individual sphere. The goodly heritage of meaningful and considerately selected chores has proven a stabilizing and vitalizing influence in the formative period of mental health development. The mental hygienic values of chores was well described by a mother. Tommy was the neighborhood pest. Flower beds suffered continually from his trespassing. She decided to give her child a back plot with a bit of garden space. His interest once roused, he carefully dug the bare spots in the grass plot and put in grass seed. He became enthusiastic over the sprouting seedlings in his garden and woe to careless feet that trespassed. Once he became a property owner himself, he began to respect the property rights of others.

L. P. Jacks states the higher aims of physical education in the new made world of leisure. "The economist predicts that the necessary work of the world will be done ultimately in a four-hour day or a shorter week. We are quite unprepared for that and the existing forms of education are doing too little. However, those of us who are in the recreation movements, are exploring the possibilities. We have not fully worked out a program for leisure occupation; we do wish to improve the general direction and to raise the recreation level to higher skill, intelligence and enjoyment."

Although he does not know what would be the final phase of his education for leisure, Mr. Jacks believes that the first should be "the co-education of mind and body—the idea of the Greeks."

"We are just taking the first steps in the right direction," he said, "and after that the rest of the way is to make a sound physical culture accessible to everyone in the community. It must be something with a finer technique than ordinary athletics or gymnastics; something like that worked out in Sweden and Switzerland."

Work and recreation mean the same to some individuals. Mrs. Edison reports that her husband, the famous Thomas Edison, when importuned to let up from his unremitting labor through some form of creation replied "I find my rest and relaxation in my work." Others may find their relaxation in physical idleness and find in this a higher form of play, even a cultural experience. Bertrand Russell explains that he was brought up in the saying "Satan finds mischief for idle hands to do"; he goes on to say, "being a highly virtuous child I believed what I was told and acquired a conscience that has kept me working hard down to the present moment. But although my conscience has controlled my actions, my opinions have undergone a revolution. I believe there is too much work in the world; that harm results from the belief that working is virtuous. The cult of efficiency has inhibited capacity of light-heartedness in play."

The modern man thinks that everything ought to be done for the sake of something else and never for its own sake. Knowledge should be considered as more than an ingredient in technical skill, but should be considered as a mental delight.

"Study contemporary science and witness the collapse of these proud structures of materialism, mechanism and determinism in which the young rebels of our cities still fondly dwell. Or contemplate the bankruptcy of modern philosophy; hear the note of pessimism, cynicism and despair on which our rationalist symphony is ending, how the whole cosmos seems to have fallen to pieces about us as we picked it apart with all the ardor of a drop of water analyzing and judging the sea. Nothing seems left to that thoroughly analyzed universe, no significance, no drama, no lasting nobility —and hundreds of writers begin to ask whether life has any meaning, any permanent worth." [4]

PLAY AND INTELLIGENCE

The teacher should never forget that it is not the activity alone but what the activity means to the child that determines its value. Play is most frequently examined from the standpoint of physical adjustment, but how can the activity be used by the child to solve his particular problem to fit into his scheme of accomplishment or to direct his aims and to socialize his impulses? In what ways is it meaningful in the child's own world? James has called attention to the fact that it is the automatic nature of the game which gives it zest. The child does not solve its problems through intelligence alone. One does not have to be over-intelligent to play. In fact, the overly-intelligent and under-intelligent children play about the same number of games, but differ in the types of games they play. The child retarded peda-

[4] Durant, W., "Is Our Civilization Dying?", *Saturday Evening Post*, May 5, 1934.

gogically takes part in more play activities of a social nature. The child may seek the capacity to get along with people rather than the academic progress which remains beyond his ability.

The child's growth can be explained in terms of mental age, educational age, social age, and so on. Doctor Paul H. Furfey has developed a concept of developmental age, "this term suggests the stage of maturity of the personality as a whole as contrasted with special types of development." [5]

It is the contention of many psychologists that certain personality elements are more important than formal education in the construction of conduct. Doctor L. Gray Studman, University College, London, suggests a personality factor termed "F" as the personality element underlying elation, self-confidence, instability, and excitability. Professor Charles Spearman of the University of London calls attention to his "G" factor which is general mind power, and ascribes it as an element in practically every mental ability. Other psychologists claim personality keys in tendencies to verbalization and perseveration. Professor Spearman emphasizes a "G" factor which he claims goes beyond general intelligence in explaining behavior. It is a mysterious factor which appears to underline the intelligence. It is something with which one is born and which no individual effort ever increases. This "G" power might be called a person's general mind power available for all his many special purposes. "It plays a large part in most mental operations, such as reasoning, and nevertheless, seems to inhere essentially in nothing more than a capacity to associate any symbol with any meaning. These factors which appear to go beyond intelligence itself are important contributions to play experiences. Pure rationalization does not give us a satisfactory educational concept of play. Mysticism is an essential element of its engrossing spirit.

Generally the alert and more intelligent child will have less conflicts in play and those he does have will be less complex. He is more able to evaluate situations, to make more accurate observations. This does not mean, however, that he will make a more satisfactory adjustment to play than the less intelligent. The emotional makeup of all children presents wide levels of diversification and many of the more intelligent children are less flexible because of emotional immaturity. It is well for teacher and parent to realize that conflicts are not always harmful, that they may have a most important role in normal development by providing the exciting motivation for the child to surmount difficulties and in this way develop most necessary qualities of initiative, confidence and disciplined aggression.

The resolution of many of the conflicts developed in play depends more upon emotional control than intelligent evaluation and can only be solved when the child has developed the ability to accept defeat. The teacher has a most important role in this educational objective. Many have conditioned their pupils to accept only success and children are kept under this constant tension to advance farther than others and since but few excel and the qualities of excellence advanced are valid only in the classroom, many disturbing and disintegrating worries are born to develop into undesirable conflicts. The little boy who has been led to play with larger boys because they are in his class at school may most naturally attempt to solve his conflict by adopting some compensatory attitude. This will assist him to explain in a way partially satisfactory to himself and his associates his failure to keep up with his playmates. He may become critical of others, he will most probably belittle other players who are mere plodders, the teachers are simply policemen who keep him in bounds. He may then evince a seeming disinterest in play as a cloak to hide his disturbing feelings of inadequacy.

GROWING INTO REALITY

Can one conceive of a higher function of play than that of lighting the highways of reality? One of the most effective contributions which play may make to more happy and normal personality functioning is through the creation of objective attitudes. The objective attitude simply means an emphasis upon things as they really are rather than upon our interpretation of them in terms of our own impulses, desires, and biases. In the child's development from self-love to greater interest, understanding and consideration for other people and other things, he undergoes as has been most frequently stated, an evolution in which the field of phantasy gradually surrenders to objective fact. In normal development, this process is orderly and the child retains some features of his imaginative reveries while at the same time learning to distinguish between the real and the ideal. Here is a most significant opportunity for the modern parent and teacher. The child should be taught that there are two kinds of separate and worthwhile experiences; the real and the unreal, the objective and the fanciful. This lesson seems simple and easy to project. It is difficult, however, because of the fact that the mother most frequently adopts a subjective attitude toward her child and an objective viewpoint toward other children; in fact all individuals retain psychic scares from an overattachment to their ego. The teacher in spite of her pride in an academic detachment will probably have a more subjective viewpoint of her own pupils as compared to her evaluation of other teachers' pupils. All individuals find some situations which they may approach with calm objective reality and other situations in which undue feelings and disintegrating emotions frustrate them. The child looks upon certain things as "mine" and views them with egotistic and subjective bias and has difficulty in thinking in terms of "we" and "they" without this subjective coloring.

This positive and negative approach is well illustrated in play. There is a tendency in many children to pay undue attention to the affective aspect of the game they are playing. You have noted many children whose spontaneity in play is seriously blocked by diffusing their energy and attention in making excuses for mistakes rather than concentrating their activity upon the actual play act. Willie will explain the reason he did not catch the first ball while going after the second one and will elaborate all the while diverse reasons for missing it by employing definite and vague excuses. All the while he is getting away from the major aim of catching the ball at the present time. He thus misses the most important aim of coming into wholesome touch with reality by actually handling the ball, by "touching the object," to use Myers' illuminating term. The positive hygienic aspect of playing the game rather than the negative aspect of making excuses, evasions and rationalizations should lend meaning and spirit to the adventure while at the same time establishing a healthy objective attitude.

In its gradual adaptation to more responsible modes of conduct, typified in a more understanding approach to reality, the child is frequently confused by so-called sportsmanship objectives in physical accomplishment. A false significance is attached to such subtle compensations in the sense that the child is through acting in a sportsmanship manner, giving up something to his opponent for an imaginary reward. These intangible qualities should be most thoroughly studied by parents and teachers and set forth to the child in an understanding manner and in an interesting setting of the game as part of the whole experience and as contributing much to the sense of fairness in strategy, an element of conduct naturally appealing to the child.

The child grows, gaining in ability to distinguish more clearly between the unreal and the real, to attach more exact and appropriate values to imagination. New and often strange values are hoped for as the child is led by rigid standardization of school and home to feel that he must become a most aggressive part of his environment, that he must attach to himself and his actions the responsibility with which some parents and even teachers invest the competitive ideal. Thus it most frequently happens that the child fails to evaluate and understand reality because of the confusion arising from foreign and detrimental aims. These resultant conflicts are often mirrored in the child's play reactions.

The child should learn to understand himself in relation to the game as a contributing part. He should not take himself too seriously nor consider his individual personality as something to be entirely satisfied. An adolescent in a fit of anger berated the physical director, telling him that he loved the game too much to see it played that way (his team was losing). He was told in reply that he loved himself more than the game and was led to understand that a lessening of egocentric self-regard was more important for his welfare than winning the game.

While Froebel, Pestalozzi, and Montessori have emphasized sense training, it has been for mental hygienists to perceive the value of this type of training in mental health development. It is a most natural thing for the child to take refuge in a self-created world of phantasy when the adult world becomes too complex for him. In coming into healthy contact with reality, a child gains pleasure from actually handling tangible things rather than attempting to approach them through abstract reasoning. Feelings of distance and inadequacy may more easily result in thinking about the ball rather than actually touching and handling it. One may develop a pathological complex in play if some situations become too heavily charged with emotion and lose their objective validity. There is probably no way in which the child touches the world in such a satisfying and meaningful manner or through a more normal approach than through suitable avenues of play. It is naturally more interested in the aggressive movements of the experience than in the deceptions, the outwitting and other aspects, often masking as refinements of modern play.

The mistake is often made by both parent and teacher of moralizing and sermonizing for the purpose of creating proper attitudes and emotional patterns. Such reaction situations cannot be easily modified by formal reasoning; the effective method must be indirect. The poise and balance which come from more effective accomplishment provides a desirable subjective approach.

In some cases the child reacts to unfavorable and unpleasant experiences by reverting to phantasy and barring these objectionable things from consciousness. This is frequently seen in a game in which the imaginative child avoids the real situation by reversion to daydreaming in which he pictures the objects which are distasteful as being removed by death, destruction or being transposed to other situations where they cannot interfere with his egotistic wants. The informed teacher showed the little boy who was desirous of "killing the ball" how to catch it so that it would not hit him and hurt him and thus produced a most elemental and hygienic attitude toward play and life as well.

The teacher may learn much from the more modern method of studying the emotions upon an objective rather than a subjective basis. Modern psychologists study the emotions from their actual expression in overt behaviour. This does not mean that the individual's description of his feeling is deemed unimportant but it does imply an increasing emphasis upon the actual end results of behaviour as explaining the nature and the intensity of the emotional states. This change of psychological method is of fundamental importance to the teacher in studying the relations of children to one another.[6]

When one realizes that many of the elemental emotional patterns of the child are formed in his early play experiences, he can understand the importance of directing these experiences in a studied hygienic manner. While the teacher cannot analyze the emotional expression of the child, his exact psychological organization, he can learn much about the child's emotional life by daily observation.

Teachers need to renovate many old ideas of child-parent-school relationships. One of the most common faults is to expect entirely too much mature behaviour from their children in all relations, including play. Many children are led to adopt a defensory attitude toward our man-made world, to make excuses, to evade, to blame others when confronted with confusing play situations. Oftentimes this attitude results from expecting too much of them, demanding mature conduct from immature bodies and unorganized minds. One should not expect unflinching firmness and consistency as part of the child's behaviour in a game since these qualities are the product of more mature experience.

In creating a more objective attitude, it is well to realize

[6] Woodward, R. S., "Contemporary Schools of Psychology," Ronald Press Company, 1931.

that sense movement provides the gateway for the early training of the child. The mental impressions are gained from object experience, from touching the object or gaining other sensory experience by taste, by smell, by hearing. Impressions of these experiences are pleasant and accurate representations of experience. The child's mind becomes like a workshop with many usable tools rather than an attic in which many things are stored in a haphazard manner for possible future use. Montessori believes that the child's interest in the make-believe world is in danger of turning him from an understanding of objective fact and may result in a loss of realizing possibilities in scientific accomplishment. This great student of child education probably refers to an excessive attachment and to morbid interest in phantasy. Modern educators feel that the imaginary creations of fairy land undoubtedly provide areas of wholesome and worthwhile exploration for the growing child and that a fertile imagination should be cultivated as an educational and personality asset. Such development, paradoxical as it may seem, may assist in creating the alert, direct, and non-evasive personality.

The objective attitude is illustrated by many expressions developed in the game; many of which show value in promoting the child into healthy and aggressive attitudes toward reality, such as "hit the ball," "swing hard," "grab the ball." The impressions which come from actual handling of the object vitalized by pleasurable emotions create more exact memory images, and assist the child in more confident and less fearful conduct. Play situations which lead toward confusion are basically wrong and may be productive of much harm. Confusion is known to be disorganizing to a balanced personality and it is frequently the first sign of mental disintegration leading to serious mental illness. Marked inability to concentrate, repeated failure in confidence, are signs of serious mental maladjustment. In cases of persistent confusion in act and attitude, opportunity should be provided for them to engage in some manual activity in which the stress is placed upon growth in skill or mere fun in activity rather than mental concentration. Primarily the reason for the confusion should be sought and any conflicts present should be resolved by a psychiatrist. An objective rather than subjective attitude should provide the aim.

Sanely directed play presents many entrancing highways to reality. It is interesting to compare the poise and healthy integration of the child musing over some simple problem presented in suitable play and the same child suffering many disintegrating reactions as he attempts to solve other problems presented as education. The boy attempting to work out an arithmetic assignment may make facial grimaces, shift position, make many muscular readjustments, depicting uncomfortable mental as well as physical attitudes. Mannerisms crop out as a result of excessive and diffused energy and the composite picture presented is that of an individual trying to squirm out of an uncomfortable predicament. On the other hand, when the child is given a task involving more simple problems in which a pleasurable play element is involved, the whole organism seems able to concentrate its energy into a purposeful and balanced effort in which the psychic qualities of incentive and motivation strike the match which unloosens appropriate and coordinated energy. Witness a child building a castle in the shining sand.

The impressionable child, so acutely sensitive to the changing world about him, does not have to be interested through artificial stimulation in playing with toys. He is conditioned to a most lively interest. Many parents observing this natural spirit in play feel that it is best to leave him alone. While

Burnham's observation, "when you are in doubt what to do with your child let him alone," has undoubted validity, the child requires understanding guidance in play and particularly in playing with toys. The first step in the child's approach to a toy is to observe it and the closely intertwined next step is to get it into action. While the teacher should be careful to allow the child much freedom in the manipulation of playthings, he should sympathetically guide the action by suggestion and example so that the child may get the greatest zest out of its widest utilization and associate pleasant sensations and perceptions with its use. The little boy who has a wagon will try many kinds of imaginable play with it. In the beginning, he will gain much pleasure out of pushing it against other objects, trying to dislodge them and knock them down. The modern teacher, who in the child's presence expresses such an action need by kicking a rubber ball may naturally redirect him into a more constructive and understanding expression of this naturally aggressive impulse. He is soon taught that it is more fun to kick the ball and propel it into the distance than to knock over the chair with the wagon. The child is shown the harmful effects to the chair, it may be broken or injured. With further guidance, the wagon is discovered to be a most entrancing vehicle to go places in and useful in exploring the child world by carrying things from one place to another. The significant thing about such an approach is that the child builds up wholesome associations motivating and surrounding his play and the inhibitions resulting from many painful contacts which are produced by ill considered play are mitigated. The child's concepts of the play world grow happily and become enlarged in more meaningful and positive patterns.

Such a view of early play experience will assist the child

to form more hygienic distinctions. He will be assisted to understand basic differences, different capacities and rights of himself and the playthings he manipulates to satisfy his early cravings. An outgrowth of this stage, will enable him to understand better personal desires in the light of the interaction of others. As he distinguishes self from others he slowly becomes aware of conflicting desires and rights of others. He distinguishes between rights of ownership, those things which are his, those things which belong to others, and those things which are jointly owned. Thus his toys connotate a wide and complex world not only of tangible things but of impulses and emotions, which, under the discerning and sympathetic guidance and help of friendly teachers and parents may be developed into most significantly powerful elements of the wholesome personality, one which is increasingly growing into reality.

BIBLIOGRAPHY

The Child's Conception of The World, J. Piaget, Translated by J. and A. Tomlinson, New York, Harcourt Brace, 1929. A sympathetic and thorough insight into the child's world of seeing and feeling and acting.

Happy Childhood, John C. Anderson, New York, Appleton-Century Co., 1933. Discusses childhood from the standpoint of an integrated and unified being.

The Management of Young Children, William E. Blatz and Helen Bott, New York, Morrow, 1930. A philosophic treatment of child training with practical suggestions. A valuable reference for play orientation.

Your Child Today and Tomorrow, Sidonie M. Gruenberg, New York, Blue Ribbon Books, 1934. A happy combination of clear cut common sense and the scientific approach to the solution of family and child problems.

The Biological Basis of Human Nature, Herbert Spencer Jennings, New York, Norton, 1930. A foundation study for the genetic interpretation of the behaviour. Material on growth processes in relationship to interests and capacity is fundamental to an understanding of the play field of the child.

Development of Learning in Young Children, Lovisa Catharine Wagoner, New York, McGraw-Hill, 1933. The child is treated as a moving entity and in relationship to the concept of conduct as a unity of mental and physical processes integrated by interest. Of significance in illuminating the psychological medium for recreation.

Heredity and Environment, Gladys C. Schwesinger, New York, Macmillan, 1933. Treats the impact of surroundings upon the nature of the child with a résumé of the status of present knowledge of eugenic experimentation. Gives an improved understanding of present and past factors entering into the recreational interests and abilities of the child.

An Introduction to Sex Education, Winifred V. Richmond, New York, Farrar and Rinehart, 1934. Treats the history, biology and psychology of modern sex education. An orientation for the teacher in physical education in administering play for mixed groups.

New Patterns in Sex Teaching, Francis Bruce Strain, New York, Appleton-Century Co., 1934. A study of parent-child sex relationships. Clear cut answers to child's questions from the viewpoint of normalizing sex into a constructive concept and function. A modern perspective for boy-girl relationships on the playground.

ARTICLES

The Definition of Introversion, Extraversion and Allied Concepts, E. S. Conklin, Jour. of Abnormal and Social Psychology, Vol. 17 (1922-23), pp. 368-377. A clear conception of these most important psychological patterns of behaviour.

Normal and Abnormal Repression, A. Meyer, Progressive Education Association, Bulletin No. 13, 1922. An illuminating discussion of the factors which enter so strongly into the mechanism of play and make it an expansive and wholesome or a restrictive and harmful experience.

Report of the Committee on Objectives and Policies of American Physical Education Association, W. W. Mustaine, Chairman, Research Quarterly of A.P.E.A. December, 1934. A most comprehensive summary of objectives of physical education for physical health, mental efficiency, social-moral character, emotional expression and control and appreciations.

Chapter III

PLAY AND BEHAVIOUR

PHYSICAL HEALTH AND PLAY

"THE FIRST AND most fundamental need of the child," states Bassett, "is physical health or as near an approximation to physical health as his structure will permit." [1] Physical health in spite of its emphasis by contemporary education as a prime objective of health teaching cannot be accorded the whole role. Mere physical strength and physical health, while most desirable conditions cannot supplant the education of the emotions. Psychologists and psychiatrists agree that the educational guidance and control of the emotional life is the most fundamental single condition for the healthy integration of conduct and while such healthful emotional functioning is dependent upon a strong physical organism, it is equally if not more dependent upon the training and the direction of the emotions themselves.

Louis M. Terman discovers five groups of children, the very superior, the superior, the average, the inferior, and the very inferior. He proposes as one of the most emergent needs in education today a differentiated course of study both in content and method for these various types. The physical factors which enter into these gradations are most

[1] Bassett, Clara A., "Mental Hygiene in the Community," Macmillan and Company, p. 210.

important. Types of play should be presented to meet the intellectual physical and personality demands of these various groups. Many terms used to describe the grade of intelligence of the child are detrimental from a hygienic standpoint. For example, a child is spoken of as dull and backward and while these terms refer in the beginning to purely mental accomplishment, they assume a much wider significance in the child's actual adjustment to other situations among his playmates. He is led to feel that he is "dumb" in play because he is adjudged dull in school. He may easily feel a sense of inability or an inferiority upon the playground, while as a matter of fact he may be neither backward nor dull, but adept and able to do these things well. He becomes inwardly resentful toward those who have lowered his sense of self-respect. No child can stand repeated failures. This exposure to repeated failures "may permanently undermine his self-respect and self-confidence, habituate him to habits of evasion, deceit, inattention or bluffing, cultivating an outlook of anxiety, hopelessness, and despair, or result in the development of unhealthy compensatory behaviour such as truancy, bullying, lying or stealing. Successful achievements within the limits of the child's innate capacity is one of the primary essentials for mental health."[2]

What the child is physically, mentally, sexually and emotionally depends in no small measure upon the function of his endocrine glands. A fundamental new principle has been added to the relationship of physiology and behaviour. Doctor R. G. Hoskins[3] informs us that the study of the endocrine glands and their secretions is "a development in the field of medicine more significant than any other since the discovery

[2] Bassett, Clara A., "Mental Hygiene in the Community," Macmillan and Company, by permission of publishers, p.206.
[3] Hoskins, R. G., "The Tides of Life," W. W. Norton and Co.

of the bacteriological origin of disease." A most entrancing vista is being opened for a study of human behaviour upon a physiological basis. A study of the glands may lead to a much better understanding of many of the child's reactions in play. The school physician will look for glandular imbalance in certain unresponsive types.

Physical health is best attained through full and unrestrained physical activity motivated by deep phylogenetic forces. "Our first happiness," says Will Durant, "is at our mother's breast; but our second is in the ecstasy of play. What purpose moves these children to their wild activity? What secret desire sustains their energy? None, the play is the thing and these games are their own reward. Children are happy because they find their pleasure in the immediate action; their movements are not means to destined ends, their eyes are shown the things they do, not the stars, they fall but seldom into wells."

The conservation of physical powers of the child is one of the serious objectives of the modern educators, especially in a time when the complexity of many requirements confuse him and make it difficult to direct his energy into the best channels. The excessive emotional tension and the high speed required to maintain our social relations and adjust our social standing, our scholastic and personal demands—all these disintegrating factors make it most important to plan a program for the conservation for physical health. Physical health, however, in true hygienic perspective, must be accepted as simply the favorable groundwork for the construction of a social personality. Mere bodily vigor does not represent the aim of the modern educator but organic health laying the foundation for the most effective development of emotional and volitional organization is the objective. All these factors: body, mind and will harmoniously integrated into a happy and effective child presents the modern trend in recreational education.

BUILDING THE STRUCTURE OF CONDUCT

How play and recreation may assist in the creation of social and spiritual type of behaviour has been largely conjectural since it has been accepted as a fact too evident to admit detailed examination. Can recreation really assist in the organization of ethical and spiritual values of the child? Physical educators have frequently erred sadly in attempting to answer this query favorably by pointing out the specific attitudes which a balanced and rational regimen of play may produce. For example, they speak frequently of the qualities of manliness and fearlessness which the player may gain from concentrating his spirit and energies in some particular game. They forget that acceptable socialized behaviour and spiritual character represent a relationship of many qualities, a mosaic of many aspects, and it is this admixture out of which emerges conduct. The play counselor often prides himself upon the open and impartial mind of the players. While this is noteworthy, we must not forget Dewey's belief that analysis is fundamentally a matter of emphasis. The child should be trained in his play experiences to find the most basic and fundamental values and relate them one to another so that spiritual understanding may be gained and the formation of strong character may be helped.

This is a subtle process but many well integrated and humane types have achieved it. Witness the buoyant, hopeful, socially considerate and yet confident child playing "with a song in his heart." Many teachers of such happily adjusted children find the answer in their own lives. As soon as the child is born his social and environmental surroundings start this shaping and adaptative process. The child's attitudes are then the outcome of interplaying impulses, of emphases and biases. These attitudes establish the balance which, as Dewey reminds us, determine the character of spiritual growth. Play projected with such an aim in mind, with due cognizance of its many weaknesses as well as strong points may be of distinct value in such a hygienic relationship.

If teachers could understand the evolution of the child's interest, they would unscreen many of enshrouded secrets of effective guidance. The child is first interested in its own body and gains elemental understanding from its developing sensation. It soon learns to love its own body and from this strongly tinctured subjective stage, it reluctantly begins to concern itself about things outside its own body, and selects weakheartedly and possibly with some reluctance exterior love objects. This transfer of interest and affection is not easily attained, and an intermediary stage in which the child is driven between love for self and love for objects outside of self becomes increasingly difficult to surmount. The ideal with which the child invests the new object of affection, is the counterpart of itself and as White observes "it falls in love with itself."

This self-love is never given up entirely. The child discovers as a result of the rebuffs of experience, however, that his own self is not the perfect organism for getting the greatest satisfaction from itself or its environment and that an overbalancing subjective emphasis results in many painful experiences. He may, therefore, readjust his conduct upon a more social level to obtain greater satisfaction if he is given understanding, guidance and has discernment. If the direction is poor, the personality inadequate, and the stress prolonged, however, he may regress to simpler modes of adaptation upon a more selfish and possibly anti-social egocentric level. The ability to centrally focus all these conflicting drives and organize his urges and capacities upon the most effective level of behaviour, is the aim of the mental hygienist and the unifying of these processes is known as integration.

"The aim of education, although often obscured," explains Burnham, "is the hygienic aim... the development of a wholesome integrated personality."[4] The most fundamental characteristic of personality is, according to Burnham, "unity, wholeness, integration, and the mark of health is integration."

Play educationally conceived offers the ideal conditions for hygienic integration. Witness a child in this all-absorbing task of play. No outside influence seems able to disturb him or redirect him from his purpose. He creates castles, forts, homes, rivers, and even the gray sky in the sand; he covers up people and things and digs them out. The serenity and poise with which he goes about his work shows the highest order of integration of mind and body and creates the most favorable condition for mental stability and mental growth. Upon the other hand, note the little boy's mother hurrying to prepare the midday lunch; attempting to do many things and think of many things at one time, under vexatious tension, bewildered, unable to relax and to coordinate and focus her activity in a quiet and effective manner. She has lost, in some way, the motivating capacity for unity, wholeness, the ability to integrate her many diverse activities so as to surmount impediments.

Teachers may be more accustomed to the term apperception to denote an understanding of experience; the more modern and effective hygienic term, however, is integration. The child grows and in the process of growth, there is added

---

[4] Burnham, W. H., "The Wholesome Personality," D. Appleton & Company, 1932, p. 407.

the imprintation of a wide, deep, and diverse environmental stimuli with many impressions being added to the unconscious self, often expressing themselves in puzzling overt behaviour. Many seemingly unrelated stimuli as the smile of the mother, the dress of his teacher, the color of the baseball bat, the complexity of his arithmetic lesson, the brightness of the day, the comfort of his clothing—these and a myriad of confusing excitants from the unconscious as well as the conscious level, emerging from our complex way of living, contribute to a pattern of behaviour circumscribing the mode and extent of his reaction to situations which appear to have little or no relations to these things.

The child develops both individualistic and social qualities with growth and understanding. Normally, the self-centered individualistic makeup becomes slowly modified in favor of the more social adaptation. The social qualities in play provide suitable relationships between the child and his associates. Some of the constructive behaviour qualities which may be developed in this way are: helpfulness, cheerfulness, kindness, friendliness, truthfulness, justice and sociability. The individualistic qualities of aggressiveness, ambition, resourcefulness, perseverance, courage, decision, self-reliance, and enthusiasm should be disciplined in play. The progression from egocentric individualism to social qualities should be the subject of educational aims, so that the desirable qualities may be advanced and the undesirable ones discouraged.

Habits of integration may be created. The child may become accustomed to repeat the automatic elements of play over and over again, gaining satisfaction from the skill developed through such routine practice and become strongly habituated to this automatic level. While these children who overly stress the motor aspect become good athletes, they may be socially dull and uninteresting personalities. Another type may simply use this reflex skill as a basis upon which to build more voluntary responses and thus integrating his play more upon the conscious level may be enabled to remain keenly sensitive to new experience. They prove most interesting and popular personalities and gain the greatest values from play experiences.

The value of play is also considered as contributing to natural self-adjusting hygienic processes. Kirkpatrick informs us that "the older schools of medicine, psychology and sociology concern themselves with trying directly to reduce extreme activities, fever, over-eating, anger, thieving; instead of indirectly through giving the body, the mind, the society a favorable environment for return to normal by natural self-adjusting processes. In general, the older methods are medical in character and are helpful only when functioning has become quite abnormal; while making conditions favorable for return to normal is a hygienic method of treatment. As the sciences of body and mind functioning develop, there will be more use for directors of physical and mental hygiene."[5]

The integrative quality of play provides an adjustive mechanism for meeting life situations and affords a more diversified and understanding approach. It may satisfy many motives which in our modern way of living cannot be completely met. "The valid concept of play," says Curti, "is consonant with Spinoza's ideal of the free man, he is the person who not only allows the simplest pleasures that come his way, but whose activity has the spirit of play, because it is harmoniously integrated in the satisfaction of the dominant ideals of the personality."

[5] Kirkpatrick, Edward A., "Mental Hygiene for Effective Living," D. Appleton-Century Company, 1934, p. 208.

The well integrated child is a participant rather than a spectator although he is taught the importance of the role of spectator in learning to understand, appreciate and evaluate the efforts of others who assume the active responsibility. "An ounce of pleasure you make for yourself," says Doctor Jacks, "is worth a ton of pleasure made for you by someone else."

How may we assist the child to build up a healthy personality balanced and well integrated? We should first examine ourselves in our professional attitudes toward our pupils for the purpose of understanding ourselves. Patry suggests "that you have a 'truth party' with yourself and also with one or more persons whom you consider your best judges and friends or perhaps a psychiatrist. This is highly desirable from the standpoint of getting objective checkups on your functioning, implicit and overt. It will also give you different points of view as well as the feeling of release of emotion and tension, and also create opportunities for encouragement." [6] Such an approach will improve our insight into the motives underlying our behaviour and assist in establishing the necessary rapport with our children.

It is very important for the teacher to understand something of the relationship of reflex and voluntary activity. These two levels of conduct in their individual and related expressions contain many significant relationships to mental hygiene. The fundamental forms of play are probably reflex, although it is difficult to determine what parts are conditioned and what parts are unconditioned. The conscious acts by repetition become reflex and reflex acts leading to wider activity may develop voluntary responses. Harm often results from making conscious experiences of acts which are essentially reflex. This often destroys the natural spontaneity

[6] Patry, Frederick L., "Mental Health," Harper Bros., 1935, p. 348.

of motor response and leads to confusion and frequently un-
happiness through blocking of smooth activity. The mistake
is also made of hurrying voluntary acts and treating them
like spontaneous automatic responses. Conscious thoughts
should be allowed for the voluntary acts and the involuntary
or reflex responses should not be overly disturbed by conscious thought or interference. The teacher should make a
special study of repetition and its effect upon the integration
of the child. All experiences which are exactly repeated
become dull as a result of the process. A healthy attitude
of persistence, however, must be awakened and fostered in
the interests of the healthful adaptation of the individual.
Our emotions become dulled, our will-power weakened by
irksome repetition. A rigid, unflinching discipline which will
face such a succession of similar experiences stolidly may
not be the hygienic method with which to deal with such
a problem. The alternation of varying experiences would
seem to be a more rational answer. Varied play may be
of assistance, for in play every situation is different. The
ball never comes with the same speed. It is never hit in the
same spot or to the same spot. The traveling object, space,
equipment and the personal equation, the phylogenetic excitation, all combine to contribute the element of puzzling
uncertainty and the variation from the preceding experience
adds interest and ardor.

"Then there should be resting points of satisfaction." He
should learn the habit of restful attention. Trying to relax
creates tension; one should stop trying. Walter B. Pitkin
suggests that we imitate a restful person, get the soft, warm,
delicious feeling of laziness. One of the oldest and best
proved tricks is to lie face down on the floor and, as the
children say, make yourself heavy—the old school yard game
of going limp all over. When you have done this well, it is

perfect relaxation. Relaxation means more than simply stretching and loosening up the muscles. The mental attitude of psychomotor integration determines its success.

In developing a wholesome integration it is important to afford ample opportunity for the child to focus, organize and develop his attention upon the immediate play act to learn and appreciate the validity of the present task. This is not as easy as it appears. Unconsciously the teacher or parent often directs the child's attention to the instructor or to himself. A further complication results because the child both consciously and unconsciously diverts attention from the play experience to himself in order to attract attention or otherwise satisfy his egocentric craving. A large proportion of the mistakes made in play are the results of such failures of integration and may lead to further mental effect as the child feels that he is losing control of the situation and cannot shape it to his liking. Such confusion may lead the child to harmful feelings of personality failure.

Children should not be forced to hurry up in play situations which are new. Such insistence will lead to a lack of balance and disrupt the necessary poise of the child. For example, in a baseball game, the child should be taught to catch the ball securely rather than to catch it with speed. With repetition the element of speed will naturally develop. Hurrying the child in untried ways, frustrates him and makes him forget necessary instructions. Fears and worries creep in to inhibit the natural spontaneity of action and demoralizing indecision may ultimately result. As the new processes are taught slowly and serenely, they become embedded in the reflexes of habit and become vitalized by pleasurable association since energy is well integrated. This natural process may lead to zestful automatic movements which the child may accomplish by little mental effort and can easily sustain with a developing happy understanding of increasing motor control and skillful accomplishment.

One of the greatest aids to integration is rhythm. Rhythm has a natural appeal to the child, whether perceived through the eye, the ear, or touch. In physical activities, the child will gradually express an individual and characteristic rhythm. The beauty of play may be largely ascribed to its rhythmic quality. The child is rebuffed by monotony but is attracted and interested in rhythm; he economizes physical effort through rhythmic organizations and both his labor and his play become less arduous. The aesthetic nature of rhythm provides a strong motivation to activity. In some subtle manner, the child expresses his unity through rhythmic movement. Just as the rhythm of the individual child creates a feeling of wholeness and exhilarating power, the rhythm of the group organization and action appeals to the child and makes him more modifiable to social influence. The rhythm of play may have the most significant influence upon the hygienic integration of the child. The rhythm of line exerts a molding influence upon art. The play and art impulse may lend themselves to integration and united make the highest integration of culture.

As stated previously, the early social adjustments of the child are tinctured strongly with egotism. These early traits of the child are not easily relinquished; he becomes self-centered and endeared to those around him who minister to his selfish cravings. The teachers have excellent opportunity to project through games a more wholesome adjustment from the self-centered interests to finer and more substantial pleasures in the group, to gradually replace self-interest with group interest, and promote advancement from self-sufficiency to partnership and sharing activities. Games can be developed very easily along these lines and methods introduced to bring about this understandable adaptation in the growth of the child's interest. For this purpose, it is helpful to introduce the play activity and develop it as a worthwhile and interesting task. Rhythmic social companionship may provide a worthwhile objective. In many cases, the egocentric integration of the child is refined by an integration upon some worthwhile task. A cooperative endeavor may present itself as worthwhile to the child and through the higher type of activity he may be able to organize and focus his activity. Many children become attracted to some group skill which play has suggested and this rhythmic human companionship may offer the vitalizing worthwhile task.

Play properly conceived may have a significant relationship to the improvement of our emotional life. Since emotions are learned, they may be unlearned. We may repeat in our play, the situations which have been provocative of desirable emotional states and thus insure a repetition of wholesome emotions. We can recondition situations which cause unwholesome release. We may change our interpretation of the emotion, we may alter its intensity, its duration and its extent. In the presence of the child we may produce the proper emotion to motivate play acts. The nervous energy which is so closely associated with unwholesome emotional release may be more naturally dissipated in play activity and while disintegrating emotions may never be completely controlled, they may possibly be modified by such palliative measures.

In order to create a hygienic basis for conduct, it is necessary that physical acts be accomplished by appropriate emotional stimulation and release. Uncontrolled emotions may cause harmful physiological reactions. For example, fear may produce destructive bodily changes as well as personality disintegration. It is important for those in charge of play to seek the hygienic body-mind relationships in which a wide category of physical activity is attended by controlled emotion, emotions which will sustain both healthy habits of play and assist in its interpretation in the light of modern and progressive education. It may thus sustain a role in preventive hygiene by emphasizing growth and modification of wholesome emotions through the natural educational progression from interest to effort.

The modern teacher who is desirous of understanding the fundamental mechanisms responsible for the mental health of the child should become acquainted with the highly important mechanisms of introversion, and extraversion. The overly introverted child gets along too well with himself. He is concerned primarily with his own selfish whims and desires, he begins to find the greatest satisfaction in his own makeup, and as a natural result very slowly retires from the necessary social contacts of the outside world. He develops into an ingrowing individual. Such increasing growth of the egocentric makeup may even cause him to further retire from reality and build up a world of self-created and self-satisfying phantasy and unreality. The extraverted child on the other hand seeks his satisfaction in experiences outside of his own self; he is the open, sociable, hardy good fellow type, he becomes interested in other people and becomes more attached to his environment. He develops into an outgrowing individual. In extreme cases this type may be shallow and lack the studious application of the introvert. The most satisfying type of conduct represents a happy balance between introversion and extraversion. The excessively introverted child may become mentally ill and the overly extraverted individual may be unable to sustain normal contact with reality. Play experiences offer ideal media for the integration of these two types into the well adjusted and social individual.

The teacher is more inclined to worry over the overly active child than the quiet and submissive individual. The overly active child may tend to disrupt classroom discipline and arrangements. The quiet introverted and submissive child may be mistakenly considered to make the better adjustment. The healthy child should have strong tendencies toward extraversions. Excessive introversion is more likely to be evidence of mental maladjustment, particularly extreme shyness, timidity and phantasy dreaming which characterizes some of these types. Normal play although it contains significant introverting elements is above all extraverting; it tends to develop the aggressive and positive character of the child.

MORALIZING ABOUT PLAY

One of the most tragically humorous acts of teachers in dealing with their pupils is to moralize about play, thus attempting to reduce it to a sort of moral specification. Children are well insulated against such contacts. The emotion and serious import with which many parents attempt to moralize about play causes children to shrink away. They appear callous; in reality, youth is not so callous as uninformed, his lack of experience makes such methods meaningless. He feels we are trying to make talk rather than action—the essence of zestful play. In the words of Angelo Patri, "all we can do about it is advise when we believe it necessary and pick up the pieces when we must." Weeping and wringing our hands drives our children away from us, causing us their confidence. Progressive educators are now generally agreed that such methods are ineffective as a deterrent to undesirable behaviour. The child naturally rebels against such superimposed morality. One playground teacher reproved an errant boy of 8 with this question, "John, who always sees you when you do wrong?" "Grandma," was the prompt and sufficient reply. The mistake is also frequently made by teachers of confusing moral qualities with mental health. The presence of moral qualities is not necessarily indicative of mental health. Unhealthy functioning characterizes mental sickness.

In attempting to sermonize about our children's play, we most frequently overwork the word "ought"; we tell them that they ought to practice more frequently and the more we employ this approach, the less likely the child is to respond. We tell him that he ought to care more zealously for his toys. These "oughts" mean in many cases that we for our own interests, want him to do so and so, and that he will peeve us, if he does not comply. Such approaches are generally met by failure and the reason is well expressed by Doctor Garry Meyers: "They may have an exaggerated faith in the word 'ought' and in the 'sense of duty.' They may overlook the power of habit. They may put all their hope in the heart of the child. They may overlook his feet and hands. The habits he soon acquires are much lower than the habits which his parents' standards call for. There grows a wider and a wider gulf between what he does and what his parents expect that he shall do. Very sensitive to their child's failure to live up to their goal, they are hurt. They fret and beg and scold. They play upon the child's heart-strings. They constantly thrust ought at him. This appeal only makes the child discouraged. 'What's the use?' he finally says, and throws up his hands. He may come to despise the goals that have always been held up to him and even to despise his parents.

"If, however, we can lead a child to feel that he ought to do as he should do, we shall have accomplished something. If we tell him to do hard things and make self-sacrifices just for our own satisfaction, we can scarcely count on good results. He must himself want to do right and enjoy doing it. We get best results as we shift responsibility from ourselves to our children for the consequences of their own acts." [7]

How much more effective it is to seek Social-Moral values in the game itself, to work out and condition situations which may develop these desired objectives. For example, good manners and courtesy, a sincerity and truthfulness, a consideration for feelings, limitations, and responsibility of others, a sense of fair play, all these are rational moral objectives of a play program conceived as an educational process. Rather than moralizing about cooperation as an abstract quality, is it not better to demonstrate in a game the value of active cooperation toward a common goal for the satisfaction of all rather than the lone individual. Cannot strong moral values accrue from companionship engendered from a friendly play spirit, "wholehearted followership, rather than unwholehearted leadership" may grow out of hygienically ordered recreation. Moral deportment which comes from self-direction and reliance, ability to accept social responsibility, may well represent a secondary educational value of play. Even a pleasing appearance of the person in play may have a wholesome though remote moral application.

[7] Meyers, G., "The Modern Parent," Greenberg, Publishers, 1930, pp. 301-2.

PLAYING WITH YOUR CHILD

It goes without saying that it is fundamentally important for teachers to find many close and sympathetic contacts with their pupils if they are to sustain a wholesome teacher-pupil relationship. If they want to really get close to the child, to understand him from this significant level of comradeship, as well as formal education, to feel the warmth of his yearnings, to understand his weaknesses, and his cravings for expression, in a word, to understand his real self, his physical, mental and hygienic self—teachers should play with their children. Educators must also learn the importance of establishing hygienic play goals. The young child cannot evaluate complex situations, he simply plays, and therefore, careful direction should be supplied. When we play with our pupils, we should emphasize playing and learning together, we should envisage the richness of the term competio—seeking together rather than against one another. We must teach our pupils to learn to find satisfaction, in nobler perspective, in doing the *larger* task rather than doing something better than someone else. We must constantly seek these new motives, remembering that the prospector finds gold more surely when he is looking particularly for gold. The child-teacher relationship in play may well typify higher cultural as well as hygienic aims, as the teacher emphasizes the beauty of the body in its active expression and by precept calls interesting attention to the fundamental fact that the body is not inferior to the mind. It is equally important to teach our children while playing with them the value of a sympathetic and discerning appreciation of the activity of others as well as an appreciation of the zest which vitalizes their own participation.

The teacher may preserve many of the old and substantial

values of the institution of the home as well as the school by playing with their pupils. The family with its many complex and interdependent functions changing so significantly in our time, offers a significant challenge to the educator, a challenge to study and understand the new relation and to discern its promise and threats in educational relationship. The place of the family in a changing society presents a puzzling dilemma to educators, psychiatrists, and child guidance experts, and others. In spite of all the influences which seek to depose the family of its traditional character, it is still a most important unit with distinctive qualities which may be employed in effective hygienic practice. "The traditional family," says Gruenberg, "was held sacred for the very reason that its protection of childhood was essential for the preservation of the race. As we see schools, public health services and other community agencies taking over more and more of these protective and educational functions, we may be led to question its continued usefulness. But is it not possible that as these are delegated elsewhere, there remain essential human values in the development of which no other agency seems likely to supplant the family? Modern psychology increasingly emphasizes that in setting a pattern of life for the child, in building up ideals of what life should be—that is, in establishing his ego-ideals—the parents remain preeminently effective. There is no evidence to support the fear that the family will not survive." [8]

If he is to render effective educational guidance, the teacher must study the parent play relationship. It is truism that the child is impressed more by what his parents do than what they say and this accounts in a large measure for the hygienic contact parents sustain to their children through playing with them. An imaginative little boy said to his

[8] Gruenberg, Benjamin C., "Child Study," April, 1934.

parent, "I know you are my father because you play with me." The protective influence of the parent as he and his child happily approach reality together provides a sense of security as well as a deep-seated understanding and love for comradeship. "Secure the love of the child," says Pestalozzi, "and his education is an easy matter."

Children—the counterparts of their parents, in a sense live double lives, one for their parents, and one for themselves. The early play-life of their children is devoted to imaginative activity and revery. A toddler may turn a stick into a big man; at the age of four he turns himself into an animal of some special kind or he may transfer himself into another person. He may dramatize any experience with new and different meanings. He may satisfy any of his play ventures by resort to a rich storehouse of phantasy creations. Many parents refuse to take part in any of these imaginary explorations of their children. His creations are sometimes ridiculed by unthinking parents or teachers. What is needed at this age is a sympathetic understanding and participation by the parent so that the child may associate the proper emotions and other desirable psychic values with these phantasy preoccupations. The child should be led to understand the rightful place of this form of play and above all, he should not be ridiculed by these creations which are real and valid to him as normal expressions of his genetic development.

The play pattern of the child is more likely to be that of the reflection of the parent and teacher. The personality manifestations of the parents especially are forcibly and at times tragically illustrated in their children's play. Parental and teacher influence exerts an intangible yet most persistent effect upon the child, attuned so sensitively to parent whims and whimsicalities and the educational requirements of a competitive school system. Fears, dislikes, peculiarities of father and mother often direct and circumscribe the normal activity in the growing development of the child. Neurotic parents more frequently have neurotic children, and conflicts of parents are often discovered in the offspring. Attempts at compensation as well as defensory acts and attitudes of the parent leave their disorganizing effect upon the struggling child. It would be very interesting to note carefully the type of parent who is most respected by their children. The housewife suffering the ennui which results from drab repetition of home routine and frequently leading to occupational diseases, can stimulate but little real comradeship in her child and is incapacitated oftentimes for real play with her child. A wise father realized he was not as close to his children as he should be. He very rarely had one of his children alone in his company, there were constant interruptions by brother, sister, or mother and no opportunity to become confidential or to establish a real comradeship. He met this problem by taking his children out one at a time on short trips in his car; this gave him opportunity for the close companionship which every child seeks in his parent.

We should not belittle the efforts of our children in play. If we treat with condescension these characteristics of early boyhood, the eager curiosity, a myth making imagination, a sensitiveness to momentary impressions, a desire to make big things and imitate things admired—we have failed to realize that these primitive traits are the potentialities of all the most lasting and constructive situations of later life.

The successful teacher will make a close study of the child-parent relationship. The parent who appeals to the child is above all an original character. Samuel Crothers delineates these characteristics which apply to the teacher also: "Incorrigibles who nurture and develop these early graces, refuse to accept hard and fast rules of adult life.

They insist upon finding time for activities that are not considered as tasks but as the glorious play of their own faculty. They see no reason to give up the habit of wonder; they are full of a great joyous impulse and their work is but the expression of this impulse. They somehow have time for the unexpected, the world is in their eyes ever fresh and sparkling." [9]

"The secret of parentage," says Will Durant, "is the ability to be young again, to throw off all dignity and degree and to play on an honest equality with the child."

The reaction of the child to parent play relationship affords many valuable clues to his personality makeup and direction, as well as usable information for the visiting teacher who is desirous of carrying out the most necessary coordination of home and school education. The child's success and failures in longings, interests, likes, and dislikes, ambitions, tendencies, his attitudes toward authority, his social and ethical standards, attitudes toward the home and other institutions, his relationship to father and mother, the economic status, his attitude toward school, his family history, sickness, academic standing, social adjustments in play, all these factors should be discussed with the visiting teacher, so as to effect the wisest utilization of his play experiences in the direction of wholesome mental health.

The teacher who desires to play sensibly and effectively with the child should be on the alert to recognize capacities and tendencies in him which will assist in the attainment of the greatest potentialities in happy social adjustment. He should be encouraged to help the teacher in choosing games and types of play which fit his own life of ability so that he may gain satisfaction by successful accomplishment and

[9] Crothers, Samuel, "Ignominy of Being Grown Up," Houghton Mifflin Co., 1908.

thus create habits of reasonable success. Above all, the play experience should make him happy as a doer with capacity for creating and stimulate him to appreciate the action of others. The gradual adjustment to higher social living should be a happy evolution, he should be encouraged to find interest in activities of others as well as his own. The emotional atmosphere should be charged with wholesome characters. Teachers should above all be tolerable, natural and human, and should respect the personality integrity of the child. The desirable behavior objectives should be alluringly attractive. Sarcasm and threats should never be employed. Above all, the experience should represent to the child a successful and happy adventure, a facing and understanding of reality without fear and subterfuge.

The teacher can only gain the highest hygienic values in playing with the pupil when he understands play as a trinity of anticipation, action and retrospection. In anticipating pleasant play adventures and in looking back to the past the child gains the fullest experience. Talking about the game proves itself to be a most important vehicle for training the child and through an examination of the parent's and teacher's talks to the child one can glean the value of the experience in hygienic practice. It is surprising how limited our conversation with our children is when we play with them. We seem to take it for granted that action is the raison d'être of the experience and that it is better to play than talk. Are we not neglecting a most fertile field of conversation, imaginative heights, of adventuresome contacts with people and things, of inspiriting and zestful topics, of richly significant talks about comradeship properly motivated while the experience is being actually lived? The child is in the mood for listening to his counselors and there is no better time to take pains to explain interesting things associated with their playing together. Why not tell our child who is playing ball with us where the ball came from, something about the store where it was bought, the far-off and fascinating lands which contributed the rubber from which it was made, and thus encourage the expansion of his vocabulary as well as his knowledge, and enlarge his scope of interest and activity as well. We too often take it for granted that the child understands, Marion L. Faegre reminds us, that only a third of one hundred five-year-old children know where coal comes from, less than one half knew what butter was made of. Play chatter should be more meaningful. It will then become even more interesting, inspiriting and socializing.

The teacher who plays with his child, unconsciously creates the necessary background of recognition which the boy or girl so much desires. What parent or teacher has not been importuned time after time by Johnnie to look at him while he throws the ball, casts his fishing line, draws a picture or exhibits other feats of childish skill, strength or dexterity? Johnnie is thus enabled to show that he is growing and developing into the rigors and capabilities of the adult made world. This aspect of school and home recognition and support is a most vital principle of hygienic guidance and practice and the hygienic picture of play is not complete without this compensating background.

In summary, the teacher who attains the most satisfactory and effective play rapport with his child will be careful to avoid the insidious temptation to set up adult standards for him to meet but will have him compete against his own capacity as the standard. He will not embarrass the child by overt or implicit references to his failures in play in the presence of others. He will be particular to preserve the natural and spontaneous aspects of recreation. He will not make the mistake of overly emphasizing the winning goal. He will encourage him to find the skills through which he can do his best in play, he will attempt to appease his skill hunger through constructive types of recreation. He will attempt to understand his child's capacity, to objectively evaluate his ability so as to stimulate and direct his progress in rational and worthwhile ways. He will encourage the child to find good in others and appreciate their activity and ability. He will understand the fundamental of individual differences and accept his child as he is. He will show faith and patience and realize that the child's unique personality is his most prized and precious possession; his play pattern should be respected and his personality rights guaranteed. Modern educators who seek such pregnant relationships in play will sustain the most happy and satisfactory role in effective child guidance.

PLAY AND CHARACTER FORMATION

Play may prove a most valuable medium for teaching and organizing character. There is probably no experience which, if properly administered, is so open and impartial, and typifies to the child such an essential and inherent honesty. These experiences give the child wholesome and unified impressions of actual living, of far zestful adventures out of which to fashion his ideals and ideas into constructive behaviour patterns, as he later develops the capacity for abstract thinking and for generalization. The child knows more about those things which he actually does; this fact is strongly illustrated among adult individuals who have become mentally sick. A number of mentally ill patients, many of whom could not even carry on a coherent conversation were requested to vote for the patient whom they considered to be the best all-around baseball player in the patients' league. Their answers showed that while they had lost touch with the many things, they were able to express a logical opinion as to the abilities of their fellow league members. All but four of sixty members in the league showed the ability to discriminate and to evaluate playing ability of those whom they had formed personal contacts with while actually playing.

Burnham [10] reminds us that three things are likely to be discovered in the personality of the normal child: 1. Some weak spot inherited perhaps or due to the solicitous hand of a fond parent. 2. Some complex. 3. Some special gift. The ideals and beliefs out of which character is largely formed are most vitally related to these personality attributes. Modern educators are calling attention to the fact that the child's conduct is more the result of the integration of these various capacities and levels of expression than the result of moral preachments. Play in its interrelationships to character formation presents many interesting lessons. Educators continually stress the readjustment of the child from levels of phantasy to more responsible modes of activity, typified in a more gradual approach to reality. The preschool child expresses himself in make-believe play; this self-expression, however, becomes more difficult as he experiences further growth. Many conventions and inhibitions curtail both the nature and extent of his play activities; he must now conform to more definite and realistic standards. This adaptation to the new existing realities is difficult for the child, and in some cases, he may seek refuge in a make-believe world. Generally, however, he will not go to this extreme, but will establish a sort of evasive type of conduct

[10] Burnham, W. H., "The Wholesome Personality," D. Appleton-Century Company, 1932, p. 665.

which he feels will shield him and excuse him from his growing sense of inability to meet the increasingly difficult demands of the new situation. Right at this point, the mental hygienist may assist in teaching important lessons in character formation. The difference between real and the ideal should be stressed, the futility of the ideal of perfection, the importance of accepting failure without undue depression, and success without over-excitement and egotistic pride. These related elements of character formation provide practicable objectives for the teacher.

In understanding the relationship of play and character formation, McDougall's [11] four steps in the building of character are illuminating. There are: First, the instinctive behaviour stage, the pain and pleasure level. Second, rewards and punishments modify these instinctive impulses. Third, the more social level in which social praise and blame influence conduct. Fourth, the highest stage characterized by idealism in accordance with high standards set up by the individual himself. It is evident that the highest types of character formation represent in their expression the final process in this evolution from instinctive individual modes of conduct to more highly socialized behaviour.

The child is largely a creature of environmental stimuli. The modern educator is getting away from the belief in the predominant influence of heredity in shaping conduct since experience shows that individuals are so profoundly altered by their surroundings. Mitchell [12] states four processes by which society shapes and alters human character: imitation, suggestion, instruction and control. Johnny desires to play ball; how would he get the desire to play this particular

[11] McDougall, William, "Social Psychology," J. W. Luce and Co., 1923, p. 106.
[12] Mason, E., and Mitchell, D., "Theory of Play," A. S. Barnes and Company, 1934, p. 251.

game? Through the desire to imitate his playmates whom he has seen playing this game. The way he plays baseball, the manner of putting on the glove, the style of his play, the associated phraseology, all are largely gleaned from a desire to imitate others. Johnny is importuned by his playmates to go swimming; he objects to them telling him what to do. A beautiful summer day, warm inviting air, and sparkling water, however, cause him to take a dip, the power of suggestion activates him. Willie tries to swim, he soon gets in water over his head and makes frantic and disorganized movements and comes out with nose and mouth full of water, discouraged and determined to keep away in the future. A few lessons of instruction in fundamental movements changes his prospective from dismay to pleasant anticipation. Johnny tries to pitch; he can not get the ball over the plate. With practice and training come the ability to manipulate the moving sphere and render it obedient to his desires and with this precision comes a happy sense of control over things outside his body. All these lessons so naturally and easily learned in manifold play experiences form much wider irradiations than is implied in these simple play activities. Distinctive teaching in character formation is supplied.

Doctor Alexis Carrel reminds us that honesty, integrity, moral fortitude can be taught just as nature reflexes are acquired by repetition, by organizing and controlling many situations producing these reactions. Character habits can both be learned and unlearned. The natural tendencies of properly directed play are most important in character education. In play thus presented, the natural impulse is to express oneself in wholesome and aggressive action, and in this accomplishment the natural disposition is to play open and above-board and not to cheat. In many other situations, however, particularly in some school situations, the child frequently finds himself the victim of unreasonable requirements and since he cannot satisfy these demands he resorts to cheating. Play properly conceived does not create temptation to react unfairly.

New interests often provide attitudes which assist in transforming unbecoming conduct into examples of desirable character. Billy was unable to resist taking things which belonged to others, his teacher met the situation by appointing him as her shopper since he had shown excellent ability in arithmetic. She gave him her purse containing bills and change and requested him to go to the store; he was surprised and asked, "Do you really mean for me to carry your purse"; the teacher answered that she knew a good arithmetic student could do her shopping as well as she could herself. Upon his return Billy offered to count the change, but the teacher told him that she knew it was correct. Each day thereafter an errand was found for Billy to do. He was sent to the bank to deposit a check. His trustworthiness was commented upon before his class and he developed into one of the most trusted students.[13]

Traits which may easily develop into examples of poor character may be changed by discovering more acceptable interests. Richard, aged 4½ years, developed an interest in matches; his mother found that she could keep this under control and did not forbid the use of matches but appointed him the waste paper burner of the household. Every morning he goes through the house collecting the waste paper from the baskets and burns it in the incinerator. He has agreed not to take any matches except to burn paper.

The conduct of the child like many other animals is largely influenced by rewards and punishments. Being unable to

[13] Child Problems, *Parents' Magazine*, December, 1933.

critically evaluate and differentiate, he requires information and guidance as to the moral correctness of many acts. He should know which acts are right by praise and commendation and moral satisfaction for these desirable acts should be engendered by adult approval rather than by prizes and medals. Conduct inherently correct is cheapened in this manner and in the long run does not bring the highest satisfaction. Upon the other hand, the doctrine of participating in a particular activity for its own sake is often meaningless to the child. From a hygienic viewpoint, it may be better in most cases not to discuss this aspect with the young child but simply to direct his play into wholesome channels and allow these objectives to develop more naturally with growth.

Punishment is a most important element in character formation through play as in other relations. The offending child who is too young to differentiate moral values should sustain pain immediately as the consequence of undesirable acts. It is as important that punishment follow anti-social conduct as it is for praise to vitalize the higher socialized forms of behaviour. The social concept may be simply explained to the child by emphasizing the fact that he cannot play enjoyably by himself, that to gain and sustain the highest satisfaction in play he must associate himself with others and that while these anti-social acts may not injure the teacher directly, they do interfere with the right of other participants and therefore are undesirable and cannot be tolerated. This may be more effective than the heavy teaching of some of our severely laced moralists. The child should be taught, however, that pain from a sense of failure to accomplish goals may have hygienic value, it may provide the burning incentive which will spur him on to future conquests. Normal playing cannot be free from discouragement and suffering may prove itself to be a most effective and sympathetic teacher. These disappointments in games, however, should not be allowed to create a cluster of painful ideas which will lead to mental conflict. It is in this situation that the hygienically trained teacher may turn personality failure into personality usefulness and success by bringing the child to an understanding of his capacity, his assets and himself and in the words of Ernest R. Groves, of "efficiently using the powers and urges of one's own personality." [14]

EDUCATION FOR PERSONALITY

*"The manner in which a child approaches a game, his choice and the importance he places upon it, indicate his attitude and relationship to his environment and how he is related to his fellow men."—*ADLER.[15]

The personality bent of the child is illuminatingly reflected in his attitudes as developed in play. His tendencies or pre-dispositions to react in characteristic ways toward play situations indicate his attitude toward more responsible adult levels. The morale and social outlook of the child may be reflected in this experience. Play may be viewed, therefore, as a medium for teaching attitudes and assisting in character formation.

One of the most valuable lessons in games is a refinement of the gregarious instinct. A social minded teacher wisely told his pupils that he could do without anything but friends. One of the vitalizing forces in a game should be the presence of friendly people. Children unconsciously crave for the

[14] Groves, Ernest R., "Understanding Yourself," Greenberg, Publishers, 1935.

[15] Adler, A., "Understanding Human Nature," Greenberg, Publishers, 1927, p. 92.

feeling of social unity which only friendship and mutual striving, cooperative and friendly effort can bring.

The attitude toward a particular experience determines the vividness with which it will be retained in memory. The child cannot be considered as simply having a good or poor memory, an alert or dull imagination, a strong or weak volition. He is liable to remember what is pleasing to him and to neglect things which disinterest him and repress things which are painful. He stores up selective images of pleasurable experience and pays but little attention to less entrancing impressions. He organizes a strong will power to do something especially dear to him. So the child finds in pleasurable games the excitation for valuable memory imprintations, image forming and volitional organizing activity. It is well understood that in his early experience, the child is most impressionable and peculiarly sensitive to the influence of his environment. Adler calls attention to the fact that the early impressions are the most lasting, the most vivid, and they establish the prototype or characteristic behaviour pattern which influences most fundamentally the future growth and behaviour development of the individual. The early play attitudes of the child may be determined to a large extent by his ability to gain satisfaction from play equipment. A little boy at the age of eight received a catcher's glove slightly large for his hand. At first, he was jubilant but after trying to use it, soon formed a dislike for this particular glove. At the age of nine, after playing with it, learning to use it and finding it of assistance in improving his mechanical skill, he stated in rather positive terms, "I like the glove now." This is a simple illustration of a fundamental lesson in the mental hygiene of play. Children learn to form a wholesome liking for things which they can understand and can utilize in their child world. In this case the glove served first to symbolize a protest against unworkable conditions. After he became more skilled in motor ways, the glove became meaningful in language of childhood's pleasurable expressions and happy aligned in meaningful association to nature's growth process. This happy association enabled the child to find pleasure in progressive adaptation to our adult world.

Emotions are a fundamentally important part of play and the attitude toward them may often determine the hygienic success of the play experience. Many faulty methods are used in the attempt to meet undesirable emotional expression. It is a common practice to say, "Little Johnny is pouting, but he will soon get over it." Thus emotional tension may be met by the child fretting, becoming worried and confused and overly agitated, and continuing until the stress wears itself out. A more hygienic way to deal with such an irritating disturbance is to direct the child into some form of big muscle play activity. Thus redirecting the pentup energy into channels outside of the child's body relieves the emotional tension so disastrous in its effect upon the harmonious adaptation of the child. Adults and children alike have found many times that disturbing internal processes may be more satisfactorily adjusted to happy external behavior through pleasurable expressive forms of play. The process allowing these emotional stresses to "mutually" wear themselves out or to dissipate through rationalization results in demoralizing worry and confusing irritation. The prolongation of emotional states after the inciting cause ceases to act provides a distinctive opportunity for psychic adjustment through the relaxing levity of play.

Teachers should observe carefully the development of emotions in play. It is generally agreed that emotions are the most significant factors of personality and represent the deepest springs of human action. Wundt's classifications of the temperaments can be seen nowhere more characteristically than in the child's play; the chloric characterized by quick reactions, the phlegmatic with slow reaction, the sanguine characterized by fast and weak reaction and melancholic with slow and sad reaction.

Angelo Patri insists upon acting in understanding harmony with our children, if we are to establish an effective emotional rapport. He reminds us that "there is a way to get along with them and a way that makes it impossible to get along with them. Rubbing them the wrong way is wasteful and irritating to both sides. The sooner we find the way their fur lies and stroke it in that direction, the sooner we find ourselves in their confidence... most children have one or more marked characteristics. It is wasteful to oppose them, unless we must. It is far better to go around their edgy places and keep a safe distance from them until we are established in the children's confidence. Then we can discuss these points on a friendly basis and may get somewhere." [16]

One of the most valuable results of well ordered play is the creation of a sense of humor. The child who does not see the many funny situations which play develops, should be taught to appreciate these wholesome experiences. A sense of humor in the successful teacher is essential, since through this appreciation a new impetus and direction from worry and morbid speculation is given. The sting is taken out of many unpleasant experiences. The child may learn to laugh with his playmates rather than against them and a spirit of good fellowship may naturally grow out of this attitude. This feeling of levity may express itself in a wider relaxation and assist the child to adopt a brighter attitude toward life in general and may provide a most valuable safety valve for many strong emotionally charged situations. A sense of

[16] Patri, Angelo, "In Harmony."

humor in play assists a child to learn about himself, to evaluate himself in a more objective light, to improve his social relations. There is a most important and fundamental difference, however, between ridicule and humor in play. Ridicule and satire may serve to lower the sense of self-respect of the child and injure his personality balance and wholesome aggressiveness.

BIBLIOGRAPHY

The Behaviour of Young Children, Ethel B. Waring and Marguerite Wilker, New York, Charles Scribner's Sons, 1929. Presents many behaviour problems of young children and, in the light of more modern psychological methods, suggests ways of meeting and understanding these difficulties.

Child Care and Training, Marion L. Faegre and John E. Anderson, Minneapolis, Univ. of Minnesota, 1930. Questions, lessons and bibliography, an orientation for a psychological understanding of physical training.

The Educational Frontier, W. H. Kilpatrick, B. H. Bode, John Dewey, J. L. Childs, R. B. Raup, H. G. Hulfish, V. T. Thayer, New York, Century, 1933. A symposium of leading authorities on the philosophy of education in relationship to social and economic developments. Gives perspective for physical education.

Outline of Abnormal Psychology, William McDougall, New York, Charles Scribner's Sons, 1926. Gives the elemental aspects of behaviour processes leading to abnormal behaviour and a perspective of value for hygienic integration.

Mental Conflicts and Misconduct, William Healy, Boston, Little, Brown and Co., 1917. Gives pregnant relationships of mental complexes to resultant conduct, uncovers traits and characteristics of significance to an understanding of play as a hygienic experience.

The Child and Society, Phyllis Blanchard, New York, Longmans, Green and Co., 1928. An introduction to social psychology giving the child's background upon which a most effective program of recreation may be projected.

The Family, Edward B. Reuter and Jessie R. Runner, New York, McGraw-Hill, 1931. Contributions from authorities upon the sociological, sexual and historical aspects of the family relationship. An understanding of one of the backgrounds for the field of recreation.

Child Psychology, Margaret Wooster Curti, New York, Longmans, Green and Co., 1930. A most comprehensive and understanding presentation of the child's mental and emotional development, clarifies the psychological field for a better understanding of the characteristics and capacities of the child for recreative activities.

The Theory of Play, E. Mitchell and B. S. Mason, New York, A. S. Barnes and Company, 1934. A comprehensive and thorough treatment of play in its educational setting.

ARTICLES

Freedom and Discipline, Adolf Meyer, Progressive Education Magazine, New York, July, 1928. A psychiatric and philosophic discussion of the spirit of freedom as an essential of rational discipline.

Chapter IV

HAPPY SOCIALIZATION

CRAMPING NATURAL PLAY

"THE IDEA THAT the need (for play) can be suppressed, is absolutely fallacious," explains John Dewey, "and the Puritanic tradition which disallows the need has entailed an enormous crop of evils. If education does not afford opportunity for wholesome recreation and training, capacity for seeking and finding it, the suppressed instincts find all sorts of illicit outlets, sometimes overt, sometimes confined to indulgence of imagination. Education has no more serious responsibility than making adequate provision for enjoyment of recreative leisure; not only for the fact of immediate health but still more, if possible, for the fact of its lasting effect upon habits of mind." [1]

The Swedish peasant, Johas Stolt,[2] exclaims: "I have known a time when young people were singing from morn to eve, they were caroling both out and indoors, behind the plows as well as at the thrasher floor, and the spinning wheel. This is all over long ago; nowadays there is silence everywhere; if someone was to try and sing in our days as we did of old, people would term it bawling." Singing is

[1] Dewey, J., "Democracy and Education," The Macmillan Company, 1921, p. 241. By permission of publishers.
[2] Lehman, H., and Witty, P., "Psychology of Play Activities," A. S. Barnes and Company, 1927, p. 129.

143

simply one of the many forms of play which have been changed or discontinued by our commercialized civilization. The suppression of natural play expression undoubtedly results in much harm to a balanced personality. Parents are constantly thwarting their children's natural play. Is it in the home, Johnny must not muss up the room, or disarrange the chairs; is it at school, Johnny must rapidly obey the regulations of the play period; is it in the community, he must not trespass upon well kept lawns. The answer that such restrictions are necessary does not alter the fact of their presence nor their cramping influence. Will Durant[3] warns us: "Let the child be happy and let us not deceive ourselves with too much sacrifice of the present to the future."

"To command a child is to arouse pugnacity and resistance; this rule is almost as certain as Newton's law of motion, and likelier to survive Einstein. Be fair to the child, earn its love, and trust, and your requests and suggestions would be more effective than commands."

The inherent expressive nature of play is in no respect demonstrated more strongly than in the spontaneous chatter of players. In a game, probably, more than almost any other experience, the child feels free to speak freely, to abandon the restrictions of conventional verbiage. He feels that he has the right to talk frankly and without reserve and without over respect to conventional niceties about the foibles, fads, weaknesses, and merits of all participants, as well as to suggest methods, strategy, revision of rules, regulations and everything that pertains to the game. The hygienic import of this is most significant; it is the one experience in which the child feels complete freedom of movement and free rein of imagination.

[3] Durant, W., "Mansions of Philosophy," Simon and Schuster, 1929, p. 239.

PLAY WAYS TO EDUCATION

"The discovery of the educational possibilities of the play side of life may be counted one of the greatest discoveries of the present day. It marks, I am convinced, the dawn of a new era in human education."—L. P. JACKS.[4]

Mental hygiene has many lessons for a general education, and particularly for play education. "If mental—hygienists are showing us one thing more significantly than any other, it is that what a boy learns in school is of really little present importance to him after his school is over and he finds himself catapulted into a social and economic and political milieu that requires of him grotesquely different kinds of reaction from those that he has been habituated by his school room career to make; in a sense more real than most of us have yet envisaged. The adequacy of the educational service for tomorrow, or more precisely of today for tomorrow must be judged in terms of the success in orienting the mental attitudes and feelings of boys and girls."[5]

While the teacher may realize the necessity of emphasizing hygienic approaches; educational practice is still dominated largely by traditional ideas which require the teaching of certain definite branches and the emphasis is still in the direction of this acquirement of knowledge and skill as prescribed in the traditional curriculum. The teacher's success is judged primarily by the pupil's acquisition of knowledge and his promotion to higher subjects and grades. It is very difficult, as a matter of practical experience, to convince teachers of the importance of making the development of

[4] Jacks, L. P., "Education Through Recreation," Harper Bros., 1932, p. 39.
[5] Averill, Lawrence A., "Mental Hygiene," October, 1935, p. 532.

personality their chief aim—when to do so, would mean that this would in many cases make it most difficult to meet the traditional standards set forth. On the other hand, the intelligent physical director, not so clearly circumscribed, can more easily be taught the necessity of wholesome development, rather than mere knowledge as valid educational objectives.

The educational significance of play is best realized when we become acquainted with some of the theories which have attempted to explain its effectiveness especially the concept which utilizes the idea play as acquired behaviour. "Play," says Dorsey,[6] "is not an instinct nor is it unique in human beings or identical in the human race; it is a form of acquired behavior. The games I play as a child or adult will be conditioned by my periods and especially by social environment. What is played, who plays, how it is played, all depend on learned habits of individual response and can only be interpreted in terms of situations, stimulus and response."

In the educational adjustment of the child through play, he should be considered (a.) as an individual with individual rights and responsibilities, (b.) as a member of society. His rights and responsibilities in play depend upon his developmental rather than his chronological age and the particular social graduation or integration present or desired.

The significance of play for education is partially explained by Curti, who describes it as "higher motivated activity which though free from conflicts, is usually though not always pleasurable." It is very probable that Curti refers only to the ideal forms of play in expressing belief in its freedom from conflicts. A more comprehensive definition is given by Mitchell and Mason, who ascribed to it as "an attitude

[6] Dorsey, George A., "Why We Behave Like Human Beings," Harper Bros., 1935, p. 353.

of mind which may pervade any human activity," [7] and they attribute its value and education to its power to interest the player, absorb his attention, and arouse him to enthusiastic and persistent activity.

Real education of the child must be unpretentious; to be most effective, it should be a subtle experience. It should be among other things a quiet assimilation and association of the transpirings around us. In conformity to this viewpoint, our children should be permitted to learn before we attempt to teach them. Happy naturalism and expansive informality precede the austere canons of precept and practice. Children often laugh at our efforts to make the unfolding of the developing flower of education a scene for sad pretentious teaching.

Educators are reminding us that children act as they feel rather than as they think, and therefore, their emotional growth exerts a telling influence upon their conduct. Play affords the stage for the development of many emotional experiences. Happy and constructively balancing emotions are most naturally developed through sane pleasurable experiences. The development of the emotions, according to the latest psychological viewpoint proceeds from the early undirected activity of the child. They are not patterned from heredity but develop under psychogenetic stimulation. At birth the child's emotions are not fixed and circumscribed but may be learned and conditioned to the interactions of self and surroundings. Emotions grow with the physical and physical development and experience of the child. [8] It is thus evident that play may be the basis for the development of early emotional growth.

[7] Mitchell, E., and Mason, B., "The Theory of Play," A. S. Barnes and Company, 1934, p. 88.

[8] Woodward, R. S., "Contemporary Schools of Psychology," Ronald Press Company, 1931.

Psychiatric studies of maladjustment have revealed many factors in conventional school methods which have been conducive to mental ill health. Types of teachers have been discovered who exert a harmful influence upon the mental health of their pupils.

Harold L. Halbrook, director of school studies for The National Committee for Mental Hygiene declares, "unquestionably, the time has come when educators and specialists of mental hygiene should collaborate in formulating a program for conserving mental health. There will be involved questions relating to the selection and training of teachers, to curricula, to mental examination of children, to arrangements for dealing with behavior and emotional problems, to recreational and avocational activities, to psychiatric social service in the schools (visiting teachers), to means for recording case histories, the vocational guidance, to the grouping of pupils, attendance, promotion, et cetera.

Many children fail to gain the necessary perspective in school. For example, John somehow is led to feel that it is most important to see and understand the academic relationships between subject and subject matter. "He is importuned to note carefully that Rome is the capital of Italy." William, however, is the only one who knew this and is led to feel a sort of pert superiority because of this special knowledge. Approbation followed as a sort of logical compensation and social as well as academic processes exert their influence. While out on the playground after school, however, this special knowledge does not serve to establish the accepted level of superiority, other forms of worthwhile conduct may be more easily established. All children crave recognition and rewards attainable by all afford the greatest hygienic usefulness. The boy who can do things with his muscle as well as his mind clamors for attention upon the basis of that accomplishment in both situations, in the school yard and on the playground. The best contribution which these agencies can make is frequently lost sight of; the qualities of social cooperativeness, of striving together and of seeking pleasure and rewards in mutual helpfulness for all. The child who is taught by example and precept to seek and to find delight in the transaction of self and others, merged in cooperative endeavor toward goals uncomplicated by purely selfish motives is on the happy highway to hygienic as well as educational play.

The child is often confused by conflicting ideals of formal education and the newer social aims. A mother asked her son Jack if he was nice to an elderly lady, the mother's former teacher; Jack replied, "not too nice or familiar, I was afraid she might say, 'Jack, say your tables.'"

Many nervous symptoms have been ascribed to the inability of the child to keep up with the conventional academic requirements. The new motive in education attempts to overcome this through a more social and less academic attitude. Our social structure contains many elements of the modern play ideal. The individual is viewed as a participant in a significant socializing game with freedom to develop; a wholesome adherence to the ideals and aspirations of others as well as his own. The social citizenship is being stressed and the socialization of strivings and group aspirations and group equalities are providing the modern motif. A social cultural ideal is also emerging. The child is being taught that wholesome activity is the nice thing to do, the proper and fashionable thing to do rather than a colorless educational or social duty. Any influence capable of favorably modifying the environment, can be aptly termed educational. Play enables one to modify the environment. In determining the educational value of exercise, the suitability of various types for various conditions must be determined. Physical exercise may in content be either formal or informal; psychically, either extraverting or introverting, in spirit gymnastic sport of rhythmics. The physical and mental makeup of the child, of course, determines his general and specific needs. Rhythmics may free the body from tension. Expressionistic, gymnastic or calisthenics may also liberate the soul. The stage and experience of the individual, motor development and skills, age, sex, intelligence, and personality needs should provide the basis for the selection of activities.

The ideal educational progression of exercise should lead from sensory to creative and cultural levels. It is most important to seek in play experiences either introverting or extraverting elements. The introverted child lays too much emphasis upon self, and the overly extraverted child is inclined to be shallow and to lay too much emphasis upon the environment; a balance between introversion and extraversion is desirable. Outgrowing and ingrowing development should be balanced. Play experiences properly selected afford ideal opportunities to stimulate the emotional subjective tendencies of the child and to develop a greater interest in him for objective values and appreciations as well. The mental hygienist is cognizant of the deep significance of these elements in promoting a balanced and effective personality in the child.

Many educators emphasize the advisability and necessity of grouping children with careful reference to their capacity; while from an academic standpoint such a grouping may have many definite advantages, it may not be the best method from a hygienic standpoint. Hygienists emphasize the fact that the best way to train a child is in specific situations insofar as is practicable. Play to be effective in this specific role must encompass many life situations or at least contain the significant elements of worthwhile life patterns. In actual life, the grouping in accordance with ability does not take place; the individual must mix in and become a part of all social strata in all sets and sorts of people. The hares and tortoises must all live together. Cooperative groups exist and function upon bases but remotely related to intelligence, economic or cultural levels. This wholesome organization thrives, since the satisfaction comes from the happy attitudinal growth rather than the ascendancy or dominance of one class over another. In this connection, however, it is important to understand that the child, particularly the instable and insecure individual, should not be placed in a too severe competitive relationship. One should condition the competitive element with a careful consideration of the child's capacity and modifiability.

Many teachers do not realize the ideal medium for teaching definite lessons afforded through the play experiences of their pupils. Under the excitement of the play experience, the child becomes more modifiable and cooperative, and is in the mood to learn and understand things associated with the pleasurable activity in which he engages. Questions about the game and related subjects find ready response. Questions of the true, false type relative to concrete situations in play should be presented, and the pupil should be questioned as to whether the situation from the standpoint of promoting desirable aims is true or false. Fallacies, misconceptions and superstitions may be made the subject of true, false type of questions and answers. Repetition for the purpose of fixing the lesson is important. Children like to talk about these things which they actually do; the act is not complete until they talk about it and the dual adventure is the valid one. Educators realize the effectiveness of making definite, purposive and systematic application of play situations so that real life lessons may be learned. The lesson ideal, however, should not destroy the play spirit. Play to reach its highest educational value must have homogeneity and suspense; homogeneity in the sense that the material acts must be unified by a purposive and vitalized pattern, and suspense to provide an inciting and exciting uncertainty.

The charm of an educational ideal calling for the balanced and all-around development of the child is contained in the classic statement of Anatole France[9] in his delineation of a young girl's education: "It is only by amusing oneself that one can learn," I replied. "The whole art of teaching is only the art of awakening the natural curiosity of young minds for the purpose of satisfying it afterwards; and curiosity itself can be vivid and wholesome only in proportion as the mind is contented and happy. Those acquirements crammed by force into the minds of children simply clog and stifle intelligence. In order that knowledge may be properly digested, it must have been swallowed with a good appetite.

"I know Jeanne! If that child were entrusted to my care I should make of her—not a learned woman, for I would look to her future happiness only—but a child full of bright intelligence and full of life, in whom everything beautiful in art or nature would awaken some gentle responsive thrill. I would teach her to live in sympathy with all that is beautiful—comely landscapes, the ideal scenes of poetry and history, the emotional charm of noble music. I would make lovable to her everything I would wish her to love. Even her needlework I would make pleasurable to her by a proper choice of the fabric, the style of embroideries, the designs of lace. I would give her a beautiful dog, and a pony, to teach her how to manage animals; I would give her birds

[9] France, Anatole, "The Crime of Sylvestre Bonnard," 1881, J. Lane (London).

to take care of, so that she could learn the value of even a drop of water or a crumb of bread. And in order that she should have a still higher pleasure, I would train her to find delight in exercising charity. And inasmuch as none of us may escape pain, I should teach her that Christian wisdom which elevates us above all suffering, and gives a beauty even to grief itself.

"That is my idea of the right way to educate a young girl."

Each child should be allowed his proper place in the game. If we view play as a slice of zestful living, we must view the players as people who act and succeed and make mistakes, but do not fail, as long as they observe the spirit of the adventure. Since play is a social exploit, the players must unite their individual contributions for the higher common good. Such a viewpoint of play emphasizes individual differences in people and accepts as valid the contribution which meets with playmates' respect even though they are not the aggressive qualities which one naturally associates with play. The boy who studies the rules and can interpret them is as necessary as the boy who can fearlessly carry the ball in a football game as is also the boy who keeps the equipment in repair and cares for the playing fields. It is a good hygienic practice for the teachers to ask the players what they consider the most important happening in a particular play experience. The acts adjudged important by the child are invested with strong emotional concomitants which give them a large place in the category of contributing elements making up the behavior patterns. Basic elements of individuality, they are important in his mental as well as physical adjustment.

Many educational practices have developed from a basic consideration of "Nature and nurture, and the plasticity of the human being" to use Adolf Meyer's illuminating phrase. Dr. Meyer, however, does not accept this basis as the most comprehensive explanation of the individual's reactions to life. He informs us that "It is *spontaneity* that concerns us vitally in practical life—that which we may expect as the person's own—with or without the help of others, and at any time, irrespective of condition. A mere enumeration of isolated capacities does not bring that to us. We are interested in what the man does 'sua sponte' as a natural rise of his own nature—be it in action or rest, effort or restraint, it is spontaneity as it is the individual's or group's own nature, as part of a course of behavior and performance in action or planning or in fancy, or contemplation of the doing of others, with action, rest, recuperation and again action, with specific temperament, disposition, inhibition or release."

In educational practice there is a basic need for a psychiatric concept of the play mechanism. Teachers have too long emphasized the environment operating with the natural endowment as fixed and definite lines circumscribing the conduct pattern of play. They forget that there is something in play which is not within the bounds of such a mechanistic interpretation. The essence of play is that the individual acts "sua sponte," he plays because he wants to, and when he wants to and as he wants to in response to an inner urge. It is this *spontaneity* which makes play an inciting, exciting and expansive adventure. Something forever fresh and new, an exploration in anticipation, action and retrospection. It is this concept of hygienic unity which invests play with its greatest importance in modern educational practice. In the words of Dr. Meyer, there is need of "an experiment in developing play as the pleasing (and preferred?) background and varied activity that transforms frozen overinstitutionalized spontaneity or misguided spontaneity... into orderly and socialized spontaneity." [10]

From an educational as well as psychiatric viewpoint, it is well to recognize that the child expresses in his play his whole attitude toward life. The phenomena of play behavior represents a colorful mosaic complicated by conflicted ideals of contemporary life. Dr. Franz Alexander finds that much anti-social conduct is the result of a clash of traditions: the traditions of independent and resourceful individualism, a national heritage from our pioneer forefathers and the complex social structure of today which tends to make the individual dependent. "The group ideal of the self-made man who owes nothing in life to anyone other than himself and the group notion of supermasculinity which make being a sissy a terror for every boy, leads many youth who are basically quiet and even of a dependent nature into attitudes and acts designed to show how tough and manly they can really be." This idea of supermasculinity, of being a real sport, of not being a sissy has led to many detrimental ideals for play. The child is by nature keenly attuned to this detrimental type of psychology which is mistakenly employed by those who are struck by its effectiveness in stimulating him to make a supreme effort, especially in some intensely competitive game. The child's sense of self-respect should not only be guaranteed but built up upon a hygienically sound substructure in which the traditional pioneer individualism and the growing interdependence of contemporary life are weighed and related so as to produce the most wholesome patterns of worthwhile conduct.

The teacher who does not make a careful study of the

[10] "Spontaneity," Adolf Meyer, privately published booklet by Mental Hygiene Division of the Illinois Conference of Public Welfare, Chicago, October, 1933.

phantasy preoccupations of the child cannot understand the psychology of play in its most effective relation to mental hygiene. These pleasurable excursions into make believe experiences allow the unconscious to break its barriers and become an important actor operating with the conscious and at times taking the lead in developing, organizing and directing behaviour. The fact that the unconscious influences conduct most significantly is well known but the nature of the unconscious is but little understood by the teacher. Experimental inquiry by the modern school of psychoanalysis is bringing to light a contour of the constitution of the unconscious, its nature and as a result of further experimental study certain applicable laws are being deduced, a consideration of which is vitally important to the teacher.

These so-called laws demonstrate first that there is no consistency in the functioning of this inner level of thought. In this type of primitive thinking, the child can believe one thing at this moment and the direct opposite the next, or he can believe two contradictory things at the same time. In this respect the unconscious is the direct opposite of the conscious. There is no logic in the mental operations of the unconscious. The second characteristic of the operation of the unconscious is the all power of feeling. Wishes and thoughts simply have to be expressed to be realized. One dreams things true. The third characteristic according to Karin Stephen is "confusion of fact with phantasy,[11] thinking with doing." This is well illustrated in the hallucinosis of the psychotic patient when fancy turns into such a vivid mechanism that it controls his entire mental process and dominates even the voluntary level of thinking. The fourth characteristic of the unconscious is the ascendancy of the importance of wish-

[11] "Psychoanalysis and Medicine, The Wish To Fall Ill," Karin Stephen, Cambridge University Press, London, 1935, p. 223.

ing over the importance of knowing. The teacher who critically examines the play of the nursery child will observe
many situations in which the child reverts in phantasy to
most interesting wish fulfillments and accepts these wishes
as objective facts. The child yearns for a doll house. A nearby
cradle which in no wise resembles a doll house is turned up-
side down by the child and is accepted as the desired object.
The wish becomes the fact. The final characteristic of the
unconscious is "the failure to distinguish things which are
emotionally similar" according to Karin Stephen.[12] The emotions strongly guide and move the child, his ideas of reality
being closely allied to the feelings of self-love and self-satis-
faction. He learns to identify things and relate them with
characteristic emotions and often confuses the feelings with
the objects. He associates father with a loving caress and
anyone who coddles him may be accepted as father. More
careful discriminations are the result of the more adult level.

These characteristics of the unconscious phantasy level will
shed much light upon the educational meaning and significance of the child's play experiences. A more adequate understanding of this primitive level of thought will also assist
the teacher of play to determine valid educational goals
toward which to direct the child's delicate transition from
phantasy to the desirable levels of more objective reality.

The psychoanalytic theory of play motivation also may
supply some clues to a better understanding of play procedures in their most effective educational application. Children
have many emotional conflicts which they attempt to solve.
Since they cannot assimilate some of these experiences in a
way satisfactory to themselves there is born a strong urge to
repeat them until they are more happily related to other ex-

[12] "Psychoanalysis and Medicine, The Wish to Fall Ill," Karin Stephen,
Cambridge University Press, London, 1935, p. 223.

periences. Unable to master these situations, the child will repeat them and oftentimes alter them until the emotional conflict is relieved or resolved. He may alter these experiences until he becomes the primary actor, the doer, rather than the recipient of the action.[13]

The psychological process of this repetition compulsion is seen in the many play activities of the child. He catches the ball which stings his hand. This situation combines a pain and pleasure sensation. He accepts it, looking forward to the experience in which he throws the ball to another who will catch it and be the recipient of the painful feeling. The situation of being the recipient of pain is undesirable to the child, however, and he creates in many instances a fantasy field to which he consigns many such unpleasant experiences. In this newly created world of fantasy, he becomes the self-appointed master and pictures himself as throwing the ball to someone else. The consignment of the whole unacceptable experience to unreality, however, is not easily accomplished. The demands of reality are insistent and ever present and command some recognition. Through modifications, adjustments and readjustments and the employment of old and new experiences, he is gradually enabled to replace the original painful situation by a new, happier and hence more acceptable experience.

The psychiatric concept which utilizes the psychoanalytic approach seeks in play: a, resocializing tendencies, b, outlet for aggressive tendencies, c, wholesome fantasy expression, d, opportunities for creative expression, development of wholesome expansive rather than restrictive trends. Such a concept accepts as basic the position that conflicts must liber-

[13] "Recreational Therapy in a Modern Psychiatric Hospital," William C. Menninger and Isabelle McColl, Occupational Therapy and Rehabilitation, February, 1937.

ate themselves in action and that play properly administered as a hygienic adjuvant provides the ideal setting for many such active procedures.

This concept takes into consideration the unconscious urges of the individual, repressed resentments, pent up feelings of dislike and hatred, feelings often disguised in the unconscious which center around protests against people and things, feelings of guilt which cause individuals to become depressed, feelings which cause the child to become overly aggressive, humbly submissive; feelings which disturb and distort normal trains of thought and the normal expression of mood and temper, feelings which overly excite or diminish volitional impulses, unconscious impressions built up through traditional teaching and the American Motif of advancement through intense competition. Such intra-psychic tensions resulting from accumulation and interaction of this material in the unconscious provides the field for the study of play from the standpoint of the psychoanalytic approach.

The psychoanalytic approach to play emphasizes the problem of socializing the aggressiveness of the child. The problem of unifying such elements of behaviour and relating them to the highest type of conduct is a most pressing responsibility to those entrusted with the education of the child. Aggressive traits and trends may assert themselves directly, indirectly or symbolically. The externalization of these inner drives can be observed in the child's play reactions and since the psychomotor field is more organized at these early levels than the mental and affective states such play expressions provide a most practical basis for the examination of the underlying motivation.

Various therapeutic instrumentalities have been employed in play activities to awaken latent aggressive trends. Doctor Louis Despert, in The New York Institute and Hospital has experimented with a most interesting method for the purpose of allowing the child to express his "Emotional trends, phantasies and his repressed desires in any number of creative forms." [14] The child, after being placed in isolation so as to create the most favorable environment for the expression of phantasy, is given a knife and cardboard. He is taught to scrape the cardboard and then refashion the shavings into some model by mixing the scrapings with glue, water and flour. A study is made of these creations of the child. The conclusion drawn from such observation is that the mental content brought out is predominantly aggressive. It appears that the "early, forgotten memories of hostile nature are thus reactivated and phantasies of aggression brought to consciousness." As previously stated, the child tends to repeat experiences involving a conflict until an adequate solution of the emotional problem is attained. He finds satisfaction out of the creative process as well as the created object and the creative ability for which recognition is sought. He is also enabled to gain insight into his reasons for doing things and the teacher is helped in discovering deeper incentives to action.

A most interesting psychoanalytic play technique has been developed through the utilization of Puppetry as a psychotherapeutic method with problem children at the Bellevue Psychiatric Hospital of New York. The idea is not to give instruction to the children in Puppetry as a prescribed handicraft. Dr. Lauretta Bender explains: "We feel that psychiatrically puppetry is beneficial in giving the child an opportunity to reproduce problems in drama form, and to react under observation to plays written by professionals.

[14] J. Louis Despert, "Technical Approaches Used in the Study and Treatment Problems in Children," *Psychiatric Quarterly*, Vol. XI, pp. 111-130, January, 1937.

The reaction is the more spontaneous because puppetry is entertainment, the immense popularity of which is due to the fact that most puppet plays are the outgrowth of folklore which extends back to the dark ages of racial development. Much of the folklore material deals with the questions of human relationships and suggests solutions, thus providing tools already partly shaped to the hands of the psychiatrist."

The following account of the procedure and application of puppetry is highly illuminating and undoubtedly affords clues to a more effective interrelation of education and psychiatric methods:

When the audience assembled in the hospital auditorium it found the first four rows of seats occupied by boys and girls, patients, from about 6 to 14 years of age. The puppet theatre stood on the stage, and a pleasant looking young man, Mr. Woltmann, was tinkering with the spot-light, which stood on a lectern. The young man turned to the children, and said, "Are you ready children?" "Yes," shouted the children. "Will you help Caspar out?" inquired the young man. "Yes!" "You bet!" replied the children. "Will you tell him what to do?" "Yes!" "Sure!" "You bet I will!" came the eager replies.

The young man disappeared into the puppet theatre, the lights went out, and the curtains parted. No title for the piece was announced because the children insist on finding out for themselves what the show is about. Thus "Caspar and the Devil" began. The following is a transcription from memory, of the play. If carefully read, it will show, first, what release it afforded the young patients; second, what an excellent opportunity it gave the staff to observe the reactions of the children, and, in this way, permit a clearer insight into their difficulties than might, perhaps, be obtained by the usual method of question and answer.

The opening scene showed Caspar's home. Mother is getting Father off to business. Exit Father. Then Mother calls: "Caspar, it's time to get up." Caspar: (off Stage) "Oooo—aahh—aaow." Mother: "Caspar, you lazy boy! Get up this minute or you will be late for school." Caspar: "I don't wanna go to school." (Audience giggles. Caspar makes more protests, but finally appears. He is not a school-boy puppet, but the conventional Caspar of the German puppet theatre. Something like Mr. Punch.)

Caspar: "I don't wanna go to school. I'm a big boy now. I want to live like a grown-up person, and do the things they do."

Mother: "You must go to school, so hurry and eat your breakfast." (Exit Mother.)

Caspar: (to the audience) "How about it, shall I play hooky?"

Children: "Sure, go on an' play hooky. Yer old lady won't find out." (I thought I heard one voice counsel "No.")

Caspar: "All right. I'll play hooky an' go to the movies."

Curtain—Scene 2—A Street Scene

Caspar: "What about that, Children? They wouldn't let me into the movies!"

Children: "Why? Cause ya old lady warn't with ya?"

Caspar: "I ain't got a dime. If I can't find a dime, I can't go to the movies."

Children: "Sell ya books!" "Swipe a dime!" "Swipe one off a kid!"

Caspar: "I see some kids playing down the street. Maybe I can get one offa them. So long, Children."

Curtain—Act III—Another Street Scene

(Enter Caspar and a girl-puppet. The latter is a realistic representation of a child.)

Caspar: "Where ya goin'?" (Children giggle. Someone says "Hey Toots!")

Little Girl: "My mother gave me a dime, and I'm going to the movies."

Caspar: (to the audience) "Shall I swipe the dime on her?"

Children: "Yes." "Go on!" "Swipe it!"

Little Girl: "Let me by. I wanna go where the other kids are."

Caspar: "Take me to the movies wit' ya."

Little Girl: "I can't. A dime's all I've got."

Caspar: (to the audience) "Hear that? She won't take me."

Children: "Grab it off her!" "Ask her to let you see it, an' swipe it when she shows it to you!" "Tell her you don't believe she's got no dime, an' make her show it!" (Caspar tries to grab the dime from the Little Girl, who picks up a stick, and begins to belabor Caspar. There is a lively fight, in which the children root for Caspar, but in vain. He is badly beaten, and the Little Girl goes off, her dime intact.)

Caspar: "O, the Devil!" (Begins to curse and swear in annoyance.) (Enter the Devil.)

Devil: "Why, Caspar, what's the matter?" Caspar: "O, my head! O, my knee! O, my back! She's killed me!" Devil: "What are you talking about?"

Caspar: "I wanted to go to the movies, and tried to swipe a dime off that kid just went outta here, so I could go, but she beat me up with a stick. O, my! O, my!" Devil: "Well, that's too bad. If you worked for me you could go to the movies every day. Say, Caspar, why don't you come and let me be your servant." (At this the children break out into a perfect storm. "Don't you do it, Caspar!" "He's fooling you!" "He'll kill you!")

Caspar: "What kind of work would I have to do?" Devil: "You could go to the movies every day, and have ice cream, and all the candy you want."

Children: (In great excitement.) "Tell him No, Caspar!" "Don't let him fool you!"

Caspar: "But what would you want in return?" Devil: "Nothing, only your soul. I'll make you King of the World, Caspar. You needn't go to school ever again. You could do just as you please." Caspar: "O, what shall I do? I want to go to the movies so bad!" Children: (In a frenzy) "Tell him No, Caspar!" "He'll kill you!"

(One voice from the Audience:) "Tell him 'Yes,' and then run out on him after you been to the movies!"

Caspar: (To the Devil) "All right, I'll work for you if you will let me be King of the World." Curtain.

Act IV—A Castle Hall

Enter Caspar, clad in a rich robe with a large gold crown on his head. He is followed by another puppet, also richly clad.

Caspar: "Am I King of the World?" Other Puppet: "Yes, Your Majesty, and I'm your Chief Noble." Caspar: "Anything I say goes, don't it?"

Noble: "Yes, Your Majesty." Caspar: "Well, then let's get busy about this movie business. I wanna do something for these other kids. Have a law passed, by order of King Caspar, the Great, that all movie houses has got to let in all the kids free of charge, from now on. If I hear of a single kid bein' charged, I'll put the movie house owners in Jail. You got that?"

Noble: (bowing) "Yes, your Majesty."

Caspar: (To Audience) "What about candy stores? Shall I pass a law on them too?"

Children: "Yes!" "Make 'em free too! Ice Cream too!" "Soda fountains too!"

Caspar: "All right." (To noble) "Take another law. By order of King Caspar, the Great,—From this day on, all candy stores, Ice Cream stores and soda fountains are to serve all kids free. An' if I hear of any of them charging any kid—(turns to audience) What shall I do to 'em, Children?"

Children: "Put 'em in Jail!" "Kill 'em."

Caspar: "All right. If the soda fountains break the law, tell the Chief of Police to come and put them in jail."

Children: "Gee, Free candy!" "Free Soda!" "Gee!"

Caspar: "Now, children, do we want to do anything about school?"

Children: "Yea!" "No more School!" "Burn down the schools!"

Caspar: "All right, no more school. Now what about school teachers?"

Children: "Kill 'em!" "Put 'em in jail, specially Miss Donovan!"

Caspar: "All right." (turns to noble) "Take a Law. By order of King Caspar the Great, from now on there will be no more school, and all the school teachers must go to jail." (Cheers from audience.)

Caspar: "Now, children, what shall we do about the Mothers and Fathers?" (Confusion follows this question, some children shouting, "Kill 'em! Put 'em in jail!" Others shout "No! Let 'em alone!")

Caspar: "Well, then, shall we do anything about the police?"

Children: (riotously) "Yea, kill 'em!" "Put 'em in jail!" "Shoot the police!" "The police is lousy!"

One Child: "Shut up. Don't you insult my Old Man!" (Caspar passes a law to do away with the police.)

Caspar: "Now! What about the Doctors and nurses, shall we do anything about them?"

Children: (in frenzy) "Yea, kill 'em! Shoot 'em! Put 'em in jail!" "Kill Dr. Rogers!" "Kill Dr. Bender!" "Kill 'em all, specially Miss Macy!" (The nurse in charge of the children's ward.)

Caspar: "How about unlocking the doors, Children? Would you like that?"

Children: "Yea, unlock the doors, so we can all go home!" (Sounds of rioting off stage. Voices of store men, movie owners, teachers, doctors, etc. shouting against Caspar because of the unsound laws he has passed in regard to them.)

Enter the Devil. Caspar: "Hey, what do you want?"

Devil: "I want you, Caspar. It's time you came along with me."

Children: "Now he's gonna get you, Caspar!" "You ought notta started woikin' for him!" Caspar: (to Devil) "But I don't wanna go with you!"

Devil: "But you'll hafta come. You promised to give me your soul if I would make you King of the World. Now you can't go back on it." (Takes hold of Caspar, and tries to drag him off stage.)

Caspar: "O, Save me! O, save me! Help! Police!"

Devil: "There aren't any more police. You had them all put in jail."

Children: "Run, Caspar! Knock him down!" "Get away from him, he's gonna kill you!" (The Devil begins to drag Caspar away, and seems to kill him, which makes the children very quiet and frightened. Voices of Mother and Father are heard off stage.)

Mother: "Where is our boy? He certainly came in this building!"

Father: "We want our child!" (Enter Mother and Father.)

Mother: "Why, there's Caspar!" Father: (To Devil) "What are you doing to our son?"

Children: (In great excitement) "Hey Caspar, here's your Old Man."

Devil: "This boy is mine now, and it's none of your business what I do with him."

Father: "Is that so!" (Both Mother and Father fall on Devil, and beat him, finally throw him in a corner of the stage,—Mother puts arms around Caspar, and leads him away. During the fight, the Children have been in frantic excitement, shouting and yelling.)

Father: (To Children) "What shall I do with the Devil?"

Children: "Kill him!" "Cut off his head!" (Father kills the Devil. Mother's voice is heard off stage, comforting Caspar, and telling him she and his father will fix everything.)

Mother: "Come on home, Papa, it's time for luncheon."

Curtain.

The children applauded, and so did the adult audience, for the play and the youngsters' reactions had, indeed, been interesting. In a few minutes, chattering like sparrows about what they had just seen, and making wisecracks back and forth, the children got up and filed out, accompanied by their attendants and nurses.[15]

While the full significance of the children's reactions are more thoroughly explained in psycho-analytic relationship,

[15] *Monthly Bulletin*, New York State Association of Occupational Therapists, Vol. 7, No. 4, January, 1937.

the parent and educator can readily perceive the effectiveness of such an approach in enabling the child to more adequately face his problems, to realize potentialities for wholesome emotional release, to gain social perspective as he sees how others solve the problems of the group, to "balance hostility by constructive love" and "to overcome aggression with love." The sense of security which comes from the subjugation of the evil by the right is an additional lesson of value to hygienic practice.

NATURAL DISCIPLINE THROUGH PLAY

The modern school will provide play for the child which is above all natural and spontaneous. The criterion of play for the child should be fun, zest and spontaneity. Dry and cold formality will chill the spirit. One should seek here neither a training in discipline nor a disciplinary process but an expansive and expressive adventure in enlarging lfe. Laxity of effort should not necessarily be praised at the expense of concentration nor should integrated behavior be necessarily set above easy comradeship. Buoyant, boyish boldness, illtimed adventurous exploits, youthful "long shots," imbalance of effort and objective, disproportion between volition and effort; all these factors should be viewed as natural and pleasurable accompaniment of the great adventure in physical, mental and spiritual growth, viewed always as an essentially expansive rather than restrictive or inhibitory process. It is neither an orderly nor a perfect experience. The ten-year-old boy who failed to take advantage of his opponent in a situation in which he could easily have done so, was commended by the teacher, "you have a love for the real sportsmanship of the game." "That is not it," he replied, "it is because I like you." Such self-imposed discipline enriched and fed by real admiration and love produces a most wholesome and hygienic obedience.

Oftentimes in play the child's undisciplined impulses crop out and these out of the clear sky reactions cause much worry and anxiety upon the part of the parent or teacher. A careful observation of some of these cases will bring to light the fact that faulty judgment rather than stubbornness or meanness is the cause. An eight-year-old boy tagged the runner in a baseball game so hard that he was hurt; upon questioning he stated that he had to tag the player hard so that the umpire could be sure of the play and could call the runner out. Further experience and training improved the boy's judgment and gave him a more hygienic insight. Other undisciplined impulses come out as a result of the immaturity of the child, leading to an imbalance between effort and objective with consequent misunderstanding.

Play is something more than an arrest of the child's turbulent power. It should carry the child deep into friendly human life and bring him back with enriched understanding and faith. Being a real slice of life, it should allow him to experience defeat as well as success. It should allow him to be wily, exultant, dejected, crestfallen, and triumphant. While giving stimulation to the imagination, it should have a growing sense of reality, of a wholesome experience actually lived rather than a book read. Its hygienic usefulness can only be realized when play is viewed not as slow but swift paced and aggressive and cleancut action leading to wholesome reality.

Unconventional conduct is a necessary part of hygienic play. The child who shouts boisterously and romps with abandon is simply feeling the expansive spirit of play and reducing it to a quiet and orderly experience under the guise of precise refinement deprives it of its birthright. The mental hygienist views with disquieting alarm the misguided efforts of parents and educators who, with the best of motives attempt to lower play to the level of adult preciseness by making it pretentious through formality, orderliness and restraint. Efforts to personalize recreation, to lift it above such dull routine and inject it with living and understanding people creates more wholesome ways of social behaving in child conduct.

In some subtle manner, at times from teachers themselves, some unfortunate children gain the idea that activity is wrong. The wise parent will be very careful to create through precept and teaching the impression in the child that activity is natural and desirable. Boys are always going somewhere, feeling an intensity to move, a pressing and compelling call. They chafe under the restrictions of suppressed activity. They can't stay still, they must do something. One never sees children completely still unless they are either asleep or physically or mentally sick. They must push on, roam up and down roads friendly with challenging activity. The gradual control which the child gains over his body and which may produce the most wholesome ideas and conceptions of discipline may be aided by utilizing happy things outside of the body, the many recreative aspects and contributions of his immediate environment.

In games as well as all other experiences, it is well to realize the relative value of leadership as opposed to commands in inculcating the better attitudes toward discipline. "All the sleeping dogs of pride are aroused against us when we give orders; at every imperative we stir up armies of defense. 'Ask and it shall be given you, command and you shall be refused.'"

The best playground is, to use Jack's significant phrase, "A playground of the soul as well as the body." A playground in which a child's creative self is enriched and which restrictions are the least. It is a playground where praise may replace blame for the purpose of forming the positive and highest character for the child. Will Durant reminds us that "censure cramps the soul and makes the imperfect task forever hateful; praise expands every cell, energizes every organ and makes even the most difficult undertaking an adventure and a victory." [16]

We should not infer from this that play represents a licentious abandon that the child's best expression is directed by the whims and whimsicalities of his self-centered nature. He needs guidance. "Every child needs authority and direction," says Doctor Frederick H. Allen. The concept of freedom to be himself in his earlier periods is psychologically unsound because differentiation has not developed in the child to the point where he has any clear conception of what is his own self. So instead of freedom, there may be confusion and fear. Direct temperament, but individuality of the person seems a biological necessity." Dr. Garry Myers states in a most illuminating fashion that much harm comes from parental inconsistencies in matters of discipline. "One reason why so many conscientious people wholly disapprove, in theory, of corporal punishment, is that most parents who punish are inconsistent in the selection of acts for which they punish and inconsistent in the application of the pain. For a certain offense they may spank the child today, or punish in some other way, and for a similar offense tomorrow may let him go untouched, depending on their feelings at the time. It seems that most punishment of children by their parents is administered merely to make the parents feel better for the moment. The average parent feels it in his

[16] Durant, Will, "The Mansions of Philosophy," Simon and Schuster, 1929, p. 239.

flesh and bones that every child needs some discipline, and he employs that 'heaven-sent' opportunity as an alibi for letting his own whims and foible and emotions run their course." [17]

How much more wholesome can be the conceptions and ideas of discipline which the child gathers from wholesome play experiences. He soon realizes that inattention may result in a loss of points in the game, possibly loss of the game itself—a loss in personal prestige. Failures to observe the honest spirit of the game may result in criticism or ridicule by his fellow players. Praise is substituted for blame in promoting morale and development. A wholesome respect for a good sportsman and submissiveness as well as aggressiveness is engendered. Natural punishment for deflection rather than retaliative punishment plants the seed for wholesome growth in ideals and appreciations of authority and discipline.

The many defects of correcting the child through discipline are evident to those who observe his mental hygienic development. Conventional discipline often defeats its own purpose. In the first place, only those who are in authority may discipline the child and he, being unable to analyze and differentiate carefully becomes hostile to many people whom he associates with teacher or parent who constantly restrict him. They set up in their own mind two classes of individuals: those who punish and those who are punished. Many confused and frustrated children relegate themselves to the latter class, and in a sort of heroic role, make friends with their delinquent accomplices. The frustrated child feels that this group are more like him and are more likely to understand and appreciate him. In this group, he may find

[17] Myers, Garry, Ph.D., "The Modern Parent," Greenberg Pub., Inc., 1930, p. 79.

the greatest sense of satisfaction and experience the encouragement denied him in the school or family relationship rather than the censure which has embittered him.

Now play is open and impartial. The authority comes not from personal whims, biases, and prejudices but most naturally from the wholesome and lifelike situations which play presents. These natural regulations are the same all the time, for everyone infraction of the rules leads to positive fair and necessary penalties administered so that the offender can understand them. As a result of this objective understanding of the essential fairness of the penalty, there is developed a sustaining respect for discipline, the fundamental element in hygienic discipline. Under such natural hygienic disciplinary conditions the child will not want to violate the ruling spirit of the game. The important thing for the mental hygienist is not that the child disobeys, but that he wants to disobey. Play may create constructive interests which provide the necessary impulses for better discipline. Harold C. Coffman relates a case in point. For sometime a gang of boys had been destroying property and had seriously annoyed the neighborhood by their nightly escapades. The mother of one of the boys was wise enough to offer a small building in the back yard to be used by the gang as a club house. The boys took great pride in fixing it up and equipped it to suit themselves. It gave them a constructive interest in property and as a result, these destructive tendencies disappeared.[18]

Teaching to be effective in creating a high order and sense of discipline should be unpretentious. The most natural and effective approach to the necessary discipline in play is for the parent or instructor to avoid the appearance of being on

[18] Coffman, Harold C., "Techniques of Guidance," *Child Study*, April, 1933.

hand to spy for discrepancies and to police the activity. Those in charge will do well to be as far away as they can so as to avoid the resistance awakened in the child so plainly seen when one stands over him to see that he does his assigned task.

Many parents and educators as well follow what appears to be the least line of resistance by using compulsion unnecessarily for small children in their play. It is both amusing and tragic to see them attempt to make their children unselfish by arbitrary and coercive measures. The more these means are employed to make the child unselfish, by the law of self-preservation, the more selfish the child will become. The wise teacher will employ methods of substitution by attracting the child to other and more social methods of play. A careful study should be made of the child's interest in ownership of play paraphernalia. Many impulsive people make the mistake of grabbing things from the child. What he has he feels belongs to him, and that he has more right to grab it from someone else than they have to take it from him. The child's feeling of property right and responsibility should be respected. Many children rightfully do not want to give up their playthings, feeling that other children will misuse and abuse them. They should be assured that their play property will be safe in the hands of others before asking them to share it and they should also be assured that it will be returned to them unless it is made an outright gift. The baby should be taught as early as possible that certain things belong to him, certain things belong to others, and certain things belong jointly to him and others.

A very serious mistake is often made in the young child's play through the misdirected application of pain. Pain should only be used to prevent the child from doing things which typify undesirable behavior, not to force children to do things which typify desirable behavior. Pain should be associated with the undesirable act, and pleasure with the desirable act. Another assistance in obtaining the cooperation of the child in the matters of direction and discipline, is to offer insofar as it is practicable alternatives especially in matters which pertain to the social graces. This plan is desirable. For example: in putting out the material for play, the wise counselor will say, "Would you like to put out the bases, or shall I," rather than employ a direct imperative command, especially to young children. A wide variety of methods should be encouraged so that through growth and experience, the child himself may learn to differentiate, select, and appreciate the best ways. The broadminded teacher will realize that unquestioning obedience is not always a virtue. A significant idea of discipline from the mental hygienic standpoint comes from its derivation that is, a follower. Children, more misunderstood than bad or disobedient, are best taught discipline from imitation. The young boy wants to be a doer, a creator, a conqueror, and the teacher must get the child's attitude in play. He must, above all, study himself in an attempt to discern what he represents to the players so as to establish the fundamental rapport in play spirit. The child should be led to feel that he is gaining an expression of himself rather than being used as a sort of mechanical instrument to carry out the directions and the prototype of the teacher.

The compensation which the child receives most frequently determines his type of emotional reaction. The commonsense teacher realizes the danger of allowing the child's satisfaction as a result of emotional outburst. Since we ourselves employ these means of obtaining our desires, it is difficult to correct them in our children. The child who makes a display of anger in a game for the purpose of obtaining his selfish desires, should remain unnoticed insofar as it is practicable. The game should continue as if nothing unusual had happened, and above all, he should not be given the desired object to quiet or appease him. Many unthinking parents will take a toy away from the child in order to punish him. Such emotional expressions as this may create in the child unwholesome associations, relative to that particular toy and may do much more harm than good. Children should not be punished for drawing their own conclusions, even though they may seem to deny some conventional principles of play. We should be careful not to say "thus sayeth the Lord, when what we mean is, I think such and such a thing is true." For the child who seeks attention by resorting to undisciplined impulses, it is a good plan to ignore infraction of the rules as long as they do not interfere too seriously with the normal obligation of the game and the rights and stability of other participants. Ignoring such deflection and giving special notice of compliance with rules and the spirit of the game will often bring this deviating type of children most naturally into line. The playground teacher who tells the parent in the child's presence of his becoming behavior in the game and omits too much of the unbecoming conduct primarily assumed to gain attention will achieve the better results.

Neither should we emphasize conformity and imitation as guiding principles in the child's play. The pupil may be forced into a seemingly exact conformity but he will attempt in his own awkward way to pay attention to his natural bent and individual pattern while at the same time preserving an artificially outward respect to conventionality. He should be allowed to show off in his play. The subtle artistry of the child's play—who can see all of its delicate shades, its revealing motif, its unfolding prospective and significant promise, its swift paced action, its growing transitional periods —all these elements gradually being built in the precious mechanism of which our boy or girl must face the exacting demands of life—his own unique personality.

Desirable behavior is sometimes attained by utilizing the stimulating aspects of play as motivation. One mother who had difficulty in accustoming her children to go to bed early made bed-time a happy occasion by playing a march tune while her children marched around the room a number of times before retiring, employing tremolo and triumphant chords. Thus the work of retiring became a play adventure.

There are many mistaken attitudes toward obedience. Our children soon realize that we frequently want them to obey because we feel they belong to us. We want them to satisfy us, to boost up our own importance. Educators should teach the children that they are asking obedience for the children's own benefit, their comfort, their safety, and their growth and individuality, that the pupil is not only to be obedient toward his teachers but toward all constituted authority, wherever vested, that such obedience above all will be evoked for reasonable things, for objectives which the child will understand and appreciate; above all, that teachers are to give as few commands as possible, that they are not to interfere with the child's own rights, that the teacher will not try to compel the pupil to do things just to satisfy the teacher's own creations of proprietorship and self-esteem. This ideal is not so easily brought about. Play offers many temptations to utilize force rather than educational stimulation as the motive power. Many look upon play as an aggressive and even boisterous adventure. Many boys and girls feel resentful because of the attitude of teachers who make them feel that they are exacting compliance because they are bigger and stronger than their pupils. This subtle feeling of dominance by superior strength produces many strange and violent repercussions often upon the unconscious level in our children.

Where punishment is necessary in play, it should be administered immediately on the spot and in understandable and direct relation to the projecting cause. It should not be deferred until tomorrow nor confused with other uncontributing causes. Harmful associations should not be established through punishment; for example, don't force a child to do something which is a necessary part of his routine, such as going to bed as a punishment for some infraction of the rules. Such a procedure may produce unpleasant associations about sleep and also confuse the child as to the normal cause and effect relationships, nor should the parent appeal to his fears as means of punishment or ridicule him. Ridicule is one of the most detrimental forms of punishment as it serves to undermine the child's sense of self-respect and worthwhileness. His future growth in confidence, understanding, and social adaptation depends to a significant extent upon the development of feelings of self-respect, his ability to meet the standards which he has set up for self-realization under the guidance and stimulation of environment and training.

Teachers who are desirous of preserving ideals of play as essentially an expressive and expansive activity are at times confused by the player who is demanding a reason for the selection of types of play and for many of the demands the teacher makes upon them. The preschool child must accept many play forms and ways which he cannot understand and which do not appear reasonable to him, particularly in the care of his toys. The parent or instructor should project the joyous aspects of the play experience so that conformity to necessary routine and regulations will be as pleasant as possible. The child who is directed to keep his soldiers in good condition so that they may be able to march forward to battle, may find this a sufficiently motivating interest. The most important factor in promoting desirable and adequate discipline is to foster in the child a confidence in the good judgment of the disciplinarian. The hygienically trained coach will try to impress the player with the value of rational authority because of the resultant product, a coordinated and effective team play. He must be sure that he is giving honest reasons, not plausible words cloaked in self-interest. There is always the child who asks questions to attract attention. Some mistaken coaches look upon answers to legitimate questions as an opportunity to exchange bright repartee, a sort of matching of wits and children soon react to this condition by becoming uppish toward authority and towards each other.

The jealous child in play presents a threatening problem demanding hygienic insight by the play counselors. It is most natural for all children to demand attention and many project this endeavor as a dominating objective in their play activities. Children of different ages, especially having different capacities and interests, experience disturbing inner feelings of jealousy as others of greater ability, due to more advanced age development, attain greater success and hence more attention. In this, as in all play experiences, explanation and guidance of the psychic makeup with its strivings and impulses is fundamental to the effective teaching of physical education as is an understanding of the factors which make up skillful performance. Feelings are more basic than motor expression. The teacher should aim to mitigate the feelings of defeat due to such inevitable comparisons, especially where children of the same family are playing together. Play should be administered so that all players may feel they are receiving their rightful share of the teacher's attention and the acclaim of the game and that their efforts are valid and productive of worthwhile results.

Those who mistakenly emphasize winning as the prime objective will find such an educational orientation most difficult to attain. The sense of personal worthwhileness and enhanced self-respect which the higher aims produce are most discernible in the players. They play with less inhibition, more spontaneously and show a more wholesome personality integration, as well as a higher degree of social adjustment to their fellow players.

The best psychic adjustments are made when the players feel that the game is being played by them in response to their individual interests and potentialities. If they are to attain this realization in the fullest sense, one must be careful to avoid an atmosphere of coercive discipline. From the standpoint of mental hygiene, it may be better to do away with many officials, particularly the overly important type. In fact, many games can be best played with the players themselves calling penalties for their own infraction of the rules. This creates a spirit of self-controlled freedom so necessary to the attainment of play as an expansive, hygienic experience.

If the instructor of recreation is to utilize the modern educational practices, he must allow the child a choice. He cannot consider the child as a tool for his service but rather as a person from whom he may request rather than demand obedience. This viewpoint will be understandable when the teacher realizes that the child interprets the game by the use of images and emotions with which he has been able to cope with an adult-made world. They gain more by requesting than by demanding and why should the teacher be different in this respect? Furthermore, the methods which the child uses in play while not invariably conventional may express his inner need and represent the desirable psychic reaction at the particular genetic stage of development. It is a common observation on the playground that the teacher who frames his desires in the form of requests gets along better with his pupils. He realizes that the child after all is living in his own world in which he has other interests and ways which are as valid, if not more so than the authoritarian commands of adults. Such an approach breeds the most wholesome discipline rooted in the fundamental qualities of mutual understanding, consideration and affection.

The play counsellor should above all attain a sound concept of discipline in relation to his field of activity. He should view discipline not as an end in itself, but as a means of teaching the children that there are more satisfying ways of behaving than giving vent to their own impulsive desires. He should also be careful not to create the impression that discipline is something due him from the child as such a viewpoint will tend to destroy the most natural expressive trends of the player, who should be encouraged to discipline himself whenever he can do so. The teacher should realize that the child not only grows more wholesomely but is so much more satisfied when given reasonable opportunities to use his own judgment. It is well to realize also that the child as well as the adult develops best under a favorable atmosphere of commendation, his motor processes are more natural and effective when his aims are attainable with reasonable effort and his endeavors are vitalized by judicious praise. Adult standards most frequently creep in to complicate the problem of discipline by creating unreasonable aims. Fatigue in either pupil or teacher does not receive sufficient study. The demands of outsiders, especially the rabid fan and other overly emotional spectators also create false aims of the all-importance of winning and disrupt the highest expression of wholesome discipline. The psychology of the child's adventuresome spirit should be examined in relation to discipline, punishment and rewards. We must accept him as a curious, aggressive and experimental individuality who is seeking in a man-made world opportunities to satisfy strong innate desires to learn. We must study his age. The very young who cannot be modified by explanation should receive physical punishment for undesirable behavior immediately upon the commission of the act so that he will relate pain with unwholesome conduct. The parent or teacher, however, must be skilled in guidance to assist the child to resent the undesirable act rather than the person who carries out the punishment. Too many things in the game should not be the cause of admonitions and punishment. The child may become confused or constantly irritated so that it will either pay no attention to the commands or will react with halting indecision and poorly integrated conduct. The painful association which the child forms should be directed toward the act rather than toward the person in authority. The child who picks up the forbidden knife and cuts his finger forms a most normal painful association towards the forbidden act rather than the person and projects a basis lesson for the teacher.

Educators may easily make a fetish of discipline. All must realize that the child must live in his own world, that outwardly imposed standards will impress him with their orderliness but that his translation of them into actual behavior comes slowly. It is only with further growth and understanding that he will approach the adult conventionalities. The daily practice of the parent will impress him more than their preachments.

An understanding of the genetic aspect of discipline will

unfold many puzzling problems. Ten-year-old Johnny who has been importuned day after day to wash his hands after playing ball, will most frequently neglect to do so whenever the parental admonition is absent. He will, however, of his own volition become most careful and meticulous about his appearance when he reaches budding-out period of adolescence. As Professor Arnold Geisel observes, "Children acquire more adult habits not only because they are trained, but because they are physically and mentally ready."

PLAY AND CULTURE

The concept of play as an inherently aggressive exploit has invested it with false implications of cultureless materialism and crude strength. Those who view it as a struggle for dominance, in which mastery is to be attained at any price cannot see through such physical relationships—the soul of the experience. Play in its higher relationships is far more than the development of the body, but is an aesthetic and cultural experience in which to use Jack's expression "the playground of the body becomes the playground of the soul."

One of the fine arts of the modern teacher will distinguish such mechanical and practical education from cultural understanding. Such practical education as Durant observes produces partial and not total men, it fails to develop the creative power in him "and to open his mind to all the enjoyable and instructive aspects of the world—an education that is purely scientific makes a mere tool of its product, it leaves him a stranger to beauty and gives him powers that are divorced from wisdom—education does not mean that we have become certified experts; it means that through the absorption of the moral, intellectual and aesthetic inheritance of our family, at last we have come to understand and control ourselves as well as the external world; that we have chosen the best among our associates both in the spirit and in the flesh; that we have learned to add courtesy to culture, wisdom to knowledge and forgiveness to understanding."

There has of late developed an emphasis upon participation rather than spectatorship upon the assumption that it is of more value to the individual to take part in play than to look on; this is probably a partial truth. While it is important for the child to express himself through participation, it is also important to learn to be an interested and understanding spectator, to be able to appreciate and interpret the activity of others. Thus, two forms of education, one for activity and one for passivity, are fundamentally important. When one understands that the onlookers will always outnumber the participants, one can understand the importance of training the former to appreciate and understand the activity of the latter. Furthermore, it is in this misnamed passivity that opportunities for cultural understanding and development are produced. The hygienic aspects are also evident since these two groups are dependent for their sustaining motivation upon the understanding and encouragement of each other.

One of the difficulties in the way of a cultural appreciation of play is the mistaken idea, that education is a superior primary function and that recreation is a secondary inferior, and less purposeful process. When play awakens the creative side of the child, it produces the highest order of education and advances to art in the words of Jacks "when it is raised to its highest excellence, its highest beauty and highest power."

The teacher who aspires to be helpful in presenting play

as an hygienic experience should have a fundamental understanding of art. She should understand that art is not the representation of nature but the interpretation of nature. The identification of art with the representation of nature has led many teachers to emphasize the mechanical aspect of the environment rather than the expression of the individuals or personality. This mistake is often made when pupils attempt to imitate objective things under the guise of artistic accomplishment. The child should be taught that artistic creations in physical expression are not photographic in the sense that he is duplicating with exactness the form of nature, but is attempting to give his own idea of nature. The function of art is the revelation of beauty and beauty is not an attribute of nature but the creation of the artist's mind. Play becomes art when it is raised to its highest beauty as an expression of the child's individuality. The mistake is made by both parents and teachers in making the child feel that artistic attempts when true to form are exact representations. The child's own individuality must be allowed expression as a fundamental requisite for artistic creation and this artistic sense must be carefully guided and developed. Little Mary of seven was making an artistic creation in the sand, she was attempting to mold these tiny crystals into her ideal of a man as typified by her father. The completed figure appeared grotesque and it was difficult to discern the features of a human being. The undiscerning adult could see no art in this and yet it was an artistic creation because it represented the child's ideal of love and beauty.

Biologically Durant believes that "art arises in the song and dance of mating animals and in their efforts to enhance with artifice that efflorescence of color and form, with which nature marks the season of love."

"Historically ... art arises in the decorative painting, coloring, or mutilation of the body among savage tribes. The dance offers many characteristic expressions of art." The skill and taste combined with other aesthetic principles to create beauty in the dance and its technique and spirit expresses itself most vividly upon the cultural level. The originality of the child must be developed in his play experiences if they are to reach the cultural level. The dramatization of poetry with expressive gestures, variation of manner and melody, rhythm, jingle or poem should be well understood by the child. The teacher should assist the pupils to give motor expression to their ideas of the poem. They should be encouraged to interpret their ideas of the jingle and thus advance from imitative to creative expression. Johnny, a seven-year old, after listening to his mother speak of the entrancing color of a bouquet of flowers observed somewhat disdainfully, "but mother, who can play with flowers." There is a lesson here; many artistic conceptions of beauty and color should follow the urge to feel, to handle, to manipulate, and acquire skill. The individual's hunger for skill, once satisfied, the appetite for the higher cultural forms of recreation may most naturally be stimulated.

The child confuses many values of cultural and sensory play; a boy of eleven, when told that some of his boyish expressions were not nice, remarked, "Yes, the poor people use these harsh words and the rich are more polite." He could not understand the difference between the refined and crude levels of society. The culture which may be developed from his own actions rather than in an attempt to evaluate the actions of others should be made more meaningful to him.

Many tastes of children which reflect low cultural levels may be attributed to faulty educational methods. A large proportion of boys have a strong liking for motion pictures of gangland. In many individual cases this satisfaction appears to result from the affronts which the characters in these pictures exhibit toward conventional authoritarian discipline to which these children feel they are unjustly subjected.

An interesting educational adventure, transforming the drab and unlovely environment into an expressive and beautiful instrumentality for learning, has been developed in a grammar school of New Jersey. A creative symphony composed of children in the third grade averaging eight years of age was organized. The instruments were made by the children themselves, under the supervision of their teacher, from scraps salvaged from junk piles. The kettle, snare and bass drums were made from an ashcan, cheese box and discarded galvanized washtub. The cymbals were made of two old lids from ashcans. The orchestra numbers among its instruments, chimes made from old horseshoes; clappers and drumsticks, made from shoe trees and knitting needles; tambourines made from pie plates with bottle tops for clappers; brass pipes tuned to scale, harmonizing with the other instruments in the orchestra; bells, made of flower pots; "Huegueras" (an instrument used in the West Indies) made of gourds filled with seeds and nut shells, beans, et cetera for Indian music; large horns and a triangle (a bent bar) plus two pot covers for cymbals. The pupils began with simple melodies which are in their own world. Their teacher explains that they naturally become interested in folk songs and musical literature. This affords a most expressive illustration of play raised from sensory to creative to cultural and artistic expression.

Play presented as a cultural expression must emphasize appreciation, the sympathetic interpretation and understanding of rhyme and music, including forms of rhythm; the contribution which nature may add to play such as an understanding and appreciation of nature's colors, forms, her fields, skies, streams, woods; personality appreciations such as an understanding of the cultural value of poise, good manners and companionship; an understanding of the beauty of freedom, the cultural poise illustrated by emotional expression and control, respect for law and love for orderly control. The cultural implications of creative and imitative activity should be stressed as well as the cultural values of discrimination, taste and judgment. Bodily vigor should be understood in its cultural inter-relationship. The fullness of body powers and fitness for tasks and manhood all have their cultural significance and promise.[19]

THE IDEAL PLAY

Parents as well as educators are seeking the ideal process which will lead to the accomplishment of definite educational and social objectives. Physical educators are seeking the ideal play. Parents in retrospection are captivated by the "heavenly elan," to use Durant's expression, of their childhood play experience. All are seeking a happy and blithe adventure in play.

The child's play should be on the "useful side of life" as Adler expresses it. To be in the most comprehensive sense a constructive and a creative activity, away from the chilling admonition of don'ts and musts, a growth of the child's spirit, a development and assurance of his own unique personality, an expressive process in which his boyish enthusiasm and developmental zest is given adequate rein and his personality rights are guaranteed.

[19] Report of Committee on Objectives and Policies, W. W. H. Mustaire, Chairman, American Physical Association, *The Research Quarterly*, December, 1934.

The child should be taught the progressive play attitude, the vitalizing play spirit which develops latent energy in certain pleasurable situations, energy which with growth and development forms valuable reservoirs of constructive force to be released into social spheres of ever widening responsibility and influence. Such a broad and significant concept cannot come from the hands of overly orthodox coaches and muscle trainers, nor from those mistaken educators who view play merely as a contributing element in physical education. Such a leader must have more than conventional training. He must be endowed with compelling gifts, the gentler spirit, high imagination, broad sympathy; and secondarily, he should be imbued with broad education and specific training in minute details and progressive methods.

Such an ideal type of activity must also rest upon a sound psychological basis, it must include an understanding of the many complicating factors, emotional, volitional, intellectual, habitual—all of which enter into and determine types and levels of conduct. Play should be studied as a way of behaving, as an expression in social deportment. It is, thus, fundamentally important that the physical educator have an elemental understanding at least of psychiatric problems. It is a deplorable condition that psychiatrists who are attempting to understand human behavior have laid so little emphasis upon the many significant psychological mechanisms which enter so powerfully into play. In going over a score of books, upon psychiatry and allied problems, I found in the index but few references to play, the closest reference in most cases being the word Plato. It is, of course, understood that happiness should represent the vitalizing force in play. The educator, however, who attempts to analyze and divide this elusive happiness element into contributing and interacting components will lose his prospective.

The world of happiness is in the individual, it is intangible. Happiness is action. Children most impatiently look upon mere thought as an artifice. Their natural expression emerges in movement.

There are five important qualities in promoting a more ideal play; first, the experience should be thoroughly honest; second, the particular play activity should be adapted to developmental age and interest; third, participants should be given the satisfaction which comes from equal chances of winning. From the mental hygienic standpoint one-sided games are harmful. Fourth, play should be presented as a cooperative social experience rather than a physical struggle for individual dominance; fifth, the objectives set forth should emphasize the group winning ideal and lasting satisfaction which accrues to the lone individual when winning with the group. Dorothy Frances Hawkins sets forth an interesting description of a highly desirable play procedure. "Last week a third grade teacher presented to me what I considered an ideal lesson. The day was bright but cold, so the work was taken in the play room. She had chosen Robert Louis Stevenson's poem, 'I Have a Little Shadow.' The sun was streaming in the window, falling in little patches on the floor. The children were instructed to stand in these patches of sunlight and with them the teacher discussed shadows—what made them—why on sunny days they were distinct and on a cloudy day hardly visible, why they were sometimes large and sometimes small. Then the children experimented in making large and small shadows. The poem was then repeated in unison with dramatizations suggested by the text of the poem with the teacher drawing suggestive motions for dramatizations from the pupils. Toward the end of the period, one of the children remembered that the groundhog had seen his shadow a few days before. So the pupils wanted to play that they were all groundhogs who saw their shadows and scampered back into their holes again. One pupil observed that when they cast a big shadow they look like giants, and that when the shadows were small, they resemble funny little dwarfs and stalked and shuffled around the room accordingly. The period ended with the game of shadow tag. I am sure that these pupils never forget the poem and the concomitant learning associated with it." [20]

Happy socialization should be achieved in ideal play. Many educators emphasize play as an instinctive expression. While the instincts which are purely individualistic bring an element of happiness, "to do things together," says Durant, "doubles their delight. Almost anything, even war is tolerable, if we are joined with others in it."

Ability to see the funny happenings in a game and a wholesome play atmosphere with a broad spirit of tolerance brings happy responses to such situations. It has been truly a saving sense of humor which transformed many naturally embittered situations into fine examples of high play idealism. Both teacher and pupil should find a relief from inner tension in an abandon of too serious and intense application so that the failures in skill may not necessarily denote failure in the more comprehensive purpose of the game itself. The alleviating sense of humor, however, should not be replaced by satire and ridicule. Play properly administered has as its primary function a recreation of the child's spirit, encouragement for initiative and stimulation for development in skills and the control of his own body so that he can more

[20] Hawkins, Dorothy Frances, "Practical Elemental School Program in Physical Operation," *Journal of Health and Physical Education*, September, 1935, p. 26.

helpfully and happily control the things that have so plentifully surrounded him.

In order to live more completely and effectively, the child needs in addition to guidance and energy of spirit, a feeling of his own worthwhileness, a high sense of self-respect and the ideal game must provide opportunity for this expression. Unwarranted censure and ridicule may destroy this fundamental need and not only discourage participation in the particular game but lower the level of confidence and aggressiveness upon which the child seeks social contact with others.

In a deep sense the child cultivates his garden through play and finds many deep and mystical meanings. There are many deep loves awakened which the child does not spoil by attempting to analyze, such as the love for green things. He will find significant opportunity in nature such as Mr. Hambidge found "it would be easy to stress a mystical element here; namely, that our love for green things, bright green landscapes, trees, grass is based on something more than aesthetic appreciation alone. That is, on an absolute dependence on green things for life itself, from the beginning of time before we were human beings. It hardly seems possible that this would not have affected our attitude and feelings—that we should not have had a love of green things woven into us, as man has love of the body of woman for equally deeper reasons." He adds this significant line "it is not really, he says, 'that this acre where we live is an enchanted acre, . . .' this is a rare thing to feel that life has the world of enchantment while it is being lived." [21]

The ideal play must enter deeply into the elemental spirit and instinctive yearnings of the child. The educator, in spite of the modern social motif, cannot deny many basic values

[21] Hambidge, G., "Enchanted Acre," Whittlesey House, 1935.

in the crowd as opposed to the community relationship. Life within the gang organization is often brusque and rough, often unconventional and to the uninitiated and solicitous parent, harshly anti-social and yet it is rich in elemental and fundamental social processes. The gang offers the restless boy what society has failed to provide and offers a challenge to education to give him something as interesting as the gang association and at the same time a wholesome outlet for his buoyant and adventuresome nature.

The ideal play must be flexible and cannot stamp as its unflinching aim some stereotype personality type as its goal. In the first place, neither psychology nor psychiatry are agreed as to the most desirable personality traits nor the best methods for achieving specific traits in character and health development. There can easily result a distorted emphasis upon the present tendency to socialize the child as fundamental as this educational process undoubtedly is. All children should not be forced to participate indiscriminately in large group activities. Individual differences loom large and threatening in educational practice and if we are to be constructive in our efforts we must take cognizance of the introspective child who is not comfortable in the highly extraverting atmosphere of the large group. We must condition our activities to his particular situation so that he may attain a satisfactory adaptation to his basic interests and possibilities. These types frequently make valuable contributions to our educational and cultural life because of their subjective integration and are more effectively as well as happily adjusted at this level.

HYGIENIC OBJECTIVES IN PLAY EDUCATION

In conclusion, the teacher will find the following hygienic considerations of fundamental import in organizing and carrying out a program of physical education for the child:

A. In the interest of mental hygienic application, play should be projected as an expansive and expressive rather than a restrictive activity.

B. While the competitive spirit should be retained it should be examined from the standpoint of its socially cooperative possibilities so that the concept of playing with and for each other may give a most wholesome social direction to the activity.

C. Many significant attitudes and traits of the child later translated into adult personality mechanisms and behavior potentialities are formed through play experiences.

D. Educational methods in play should emphasize the hygienic motif which ascribes a greater role to the emotions than to the intelligence while at the same time stimulating and organizing wholesome mental functioning.

E. Educational methods should seek to establish normal associations between play acts and motivation so that the most wholesome mental images may be formed to vitalize and stabilize child and adult conduct. It is what the child thinks of the activity which is hygienically significant.

F. Play should be examined as to its possibilities in the construction of more highly socialized concepts, and in the sublimation of undesirable behavior traits.

G. Play should be organized and presented as education

and educational methods should be so formulated as to preserve the automatic zest in play and, at the same time, provide the motivation to higher social appreciations and adaptations.

H. The wholesome play interests of the child should be educationally directed so as to make him more modifiable to constructive social and physical adjustments.

I. The psychic as well as the physical constitution of the child should be studied in its broad relationship to education and its more specific applicaton to hygienic practise.

J. Desirable conduct should be viewed as a unity, an integration of the many natures and capacities and interests of the individual; an integration upon the biological and social level.

K. The psychic progression of the child from the egocentric level of self-love to the altruistic level of more adequate social understanding, striving and appreciation should be carefully studied by the teacher for the possible adjuvants to be found in physical education.

L. The psychic energy generated by the tensions resulting from the child's attempts to satisfy himself and also the higher ideals of both a social and competitive society should be carefully considered by the teacher with a view to the utilization and direction of these potentialities into the most wholesome channels of conduct.

M. The false implications of the inferiority of the body to the mind and, as a result, the loss of prestige of the large muscle activities as compared to purely intellectual accomplishments should be corrected.

N. Individual differences loom large in hygienic practise

and the standards for accomplishment and recognition should be based upon the child's individual capacity rather than the ability of someone else or the rigid standards of school uniformity.

O. A healthy psychic constitution for the child is built upon the psychological foundation of self-respect. The child cherishes above all his unique pattern of behavior and is most happy when he can prove the worthwhileness of his personality to an adult world which he most frequently envisages as skeptical of his worth. The hygienic implications of this are obvious. The teacher of physical education should assist the child to form an acceptable concept of the most effective personality and aid him in establishing it and proving its validity in a cooperative and yet competitive society.

BIBLIOGRAPHY

Social Development in Young Children, Susan Isaacs, New York, Harcourt, Brace, 1933. A contribution from the psychoanalytic viewpoint, of the social and sexual unfolding and development. Illuminates the social reactions of children in play.

Everyday Problems of The Everyday Child, Douglas A. Thom, New York, Appleton-Century Co., 1927. A lucid presentation of the psychiatric aspects of child growth and training. An elemental understanding of the psychiatric approach is fundamental for the teacher of physical education.

Home Guidance for Young Children, Grace Langdon, New York, John Day, 1931. Some very interesting and clear cut examples of the utilization of effective educational methods. Assists the teacher to discern situations and factors of mental hygienic import.

Our Children: A Handbook for Parents, edited by Dorothy Canfield Fisher and Sidonie M. Gruenberg, New York, Viking Press,

1932. A summary by thirty authorities of the best current knowledge about child health and development, considering the child in the home, school and outside world. The playground teacher seeking mental health in his play projects will find much of value in this comprehensive contribution.

Guidance of Childhood and Youth, edited by Benjamin C. Greenberg, New York, Macmillan, 1926. The Child Study Association presents a source book of reading touching upon many phases of child development which will be of interest and value to the teacher seeking mental health contacts through recreation.

Normal Youth and Its Everyday Problems, Douglas A. Thom, New York, D. Appleton-Century, 1932. A nontechnical and lucid discussion of problems in personality from an educational-psychiatric angle which will enable the teacher to project lessons through play for wholesome personality development and appreciation.

Education Through Recreation, L. P. Jacks, New York, Harper and Brothers, 1932. A most excellent philosophical treatment of the social and spiritual values in recreation.

Mental Hygiene in the Community, Clara Bassett, New York, The Macmillan Co., 1934. A broad picture of the modern status and functioning of mental hygiene in society with pertinent information for the teacher.

ARTICLES

Discipline Devices, Rewards. Discipline Devices, Punishment, Child Study Association, 1931. An authoritative discussion of these devices and their effect upon personality. Of much value to the teacher in evaluating the wholesome motivating character of these methods.

INDEX